# HOW TO FOLD 2

## 100 More great folding ideas for:

Advertising Agencies
Advertising Managers
Art Directors
Binderies
Direct Mail Managers
Graphic Designers
Marketing Directors
Printers
Production Managers
Sales Promotion Managers

Written and Compiled by
## Larry Withers

Art Direction Book Company, Inc.

As all ways,
Holly

ISBN-0-88108-196-5
LCC#93-71483

Copyright Larry Withers 1996

First Printing, 1996

Art Direction Book Company, Inc.
456 Glenbrook Road
Glenbrook, CT 06906

# Table of Contents

# Introduction

As I was putting the finishing touches on How To Fold volume one, I thought I had truly exhausted the subject. I mean, how many more folding ideas could their be? Now only three years later and I'm putting the finishing touches on How To Fold 2, one hundred more unique folding ideas. The combination of these two books creates the single greatest source of folding designs known to that special race *homo graphis*.

The layout and design of these two books is very much the same, although there are some differences (improvements) between this and the first volume. Many of the fold ideas in this new book are more advanced than the first book, some requiring special die-cuts and some handwork.

In addition, at the top of each page are several check boxes that tells the reader at a glance whether the design requires text and/or cover stock, if there is any handwork required in assembling the piece, if the fold involves gluing or taping, and which designs have special die-cuts.

Generally, you will find a grid in the lower right hand corner of each page showing the flat dimensions of the folding design. Each box in the grid equals one inch. All measures are approximations and should not be used as a template for production of mechanicals. Rather, you should check with your printer or bindery for recommended specifications for measurement and exact stock. And as before you, your printer, or your paper supplier should provide a mock-up with the exact measurements of the final printed piece.

Finally, there are several pages at the end of the book provided for your own unique designs.

Good luck, and good folding,

Larry Withers

## Folder with BRC

☑ Cover Stock  ☑ Handwork  ☐ Glueing  ☑ Die-Cut

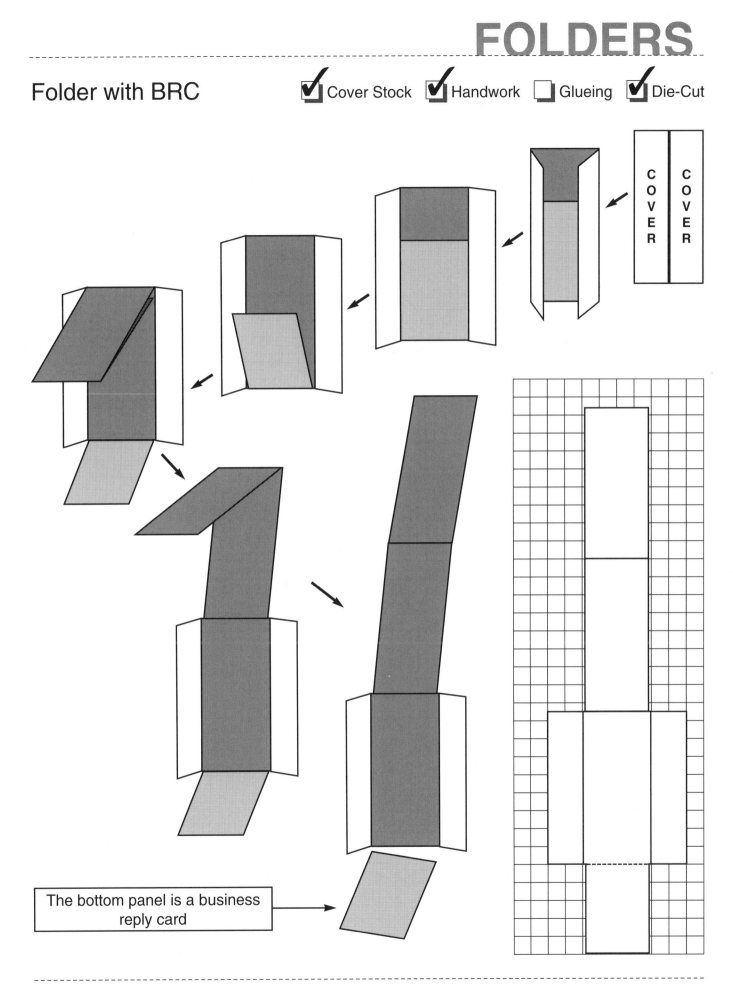

The bottom panel is a business reply card

# Folder with Postcards

☑ Cover Stock  ☑ Handwork  ☐ Glueing  ☐ Die-Cut

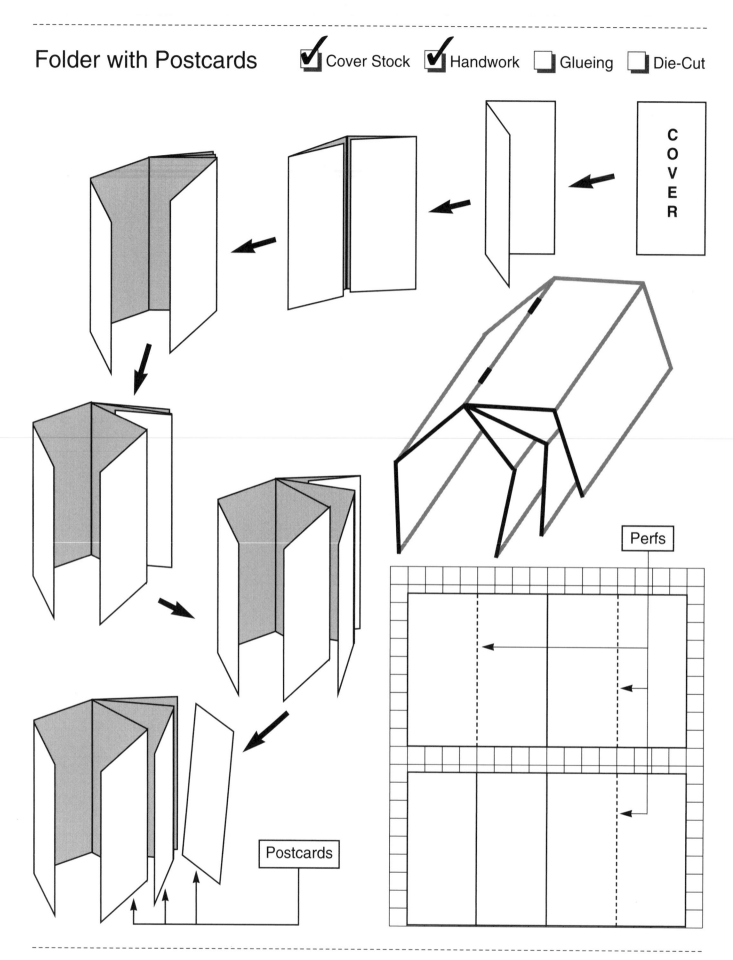

COVER

Perfs

Postcards

# Double Barn Door Folder

☑ Cover Stock  ☑ Handwork  ☐ Glueing  ☑ Die-Cut

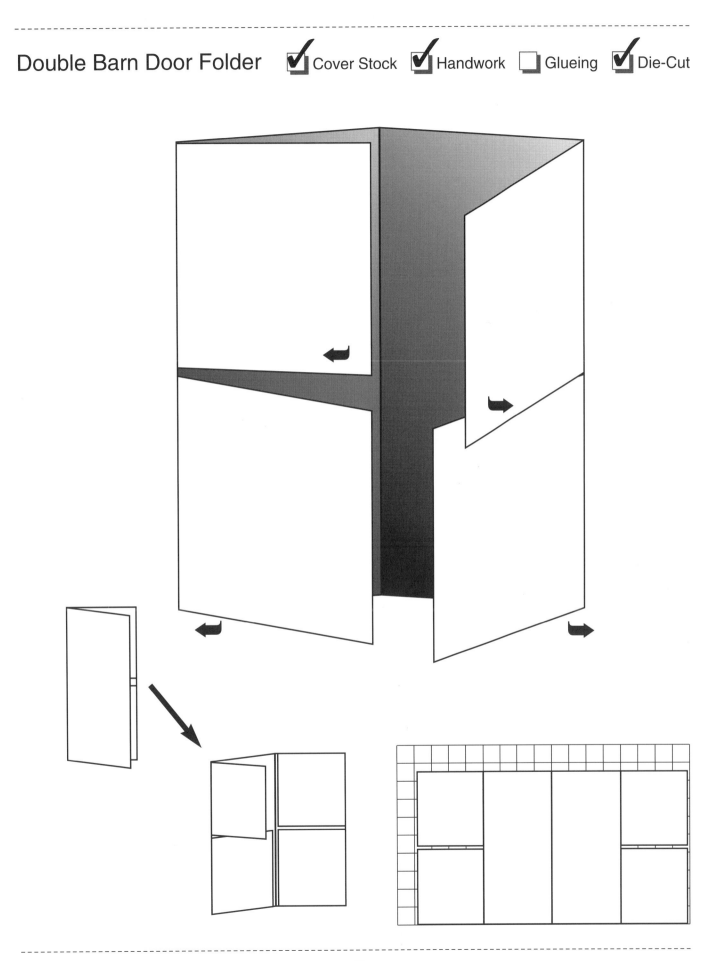

# Back/Front Folder

☑ Cover Stock  ☑ Handwork  ☐ Glueing  ☐ Die-Cut

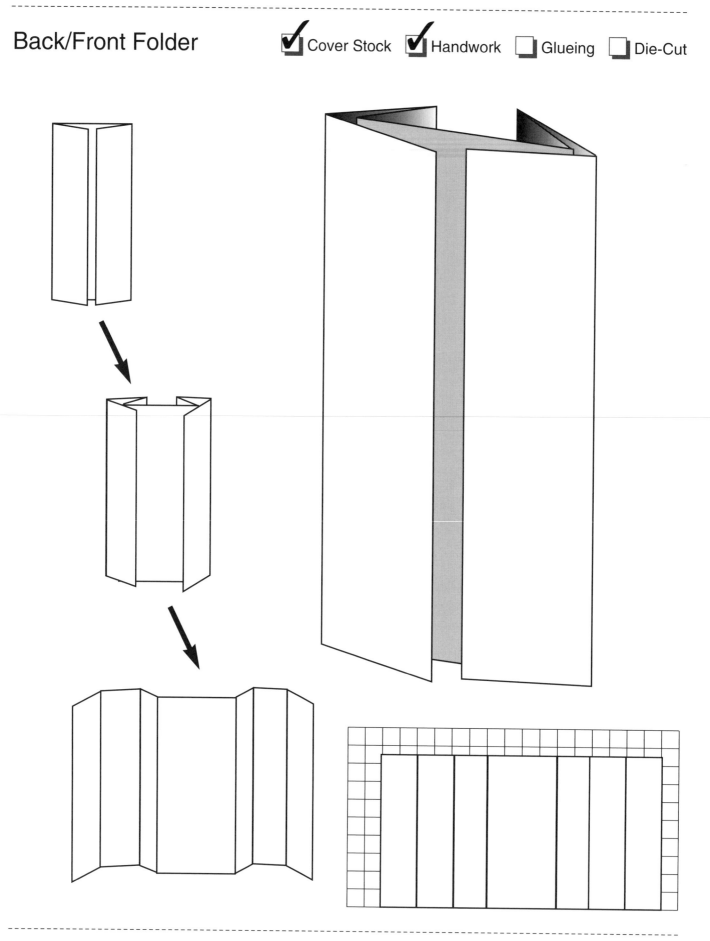

# Side Pop-Out Folder

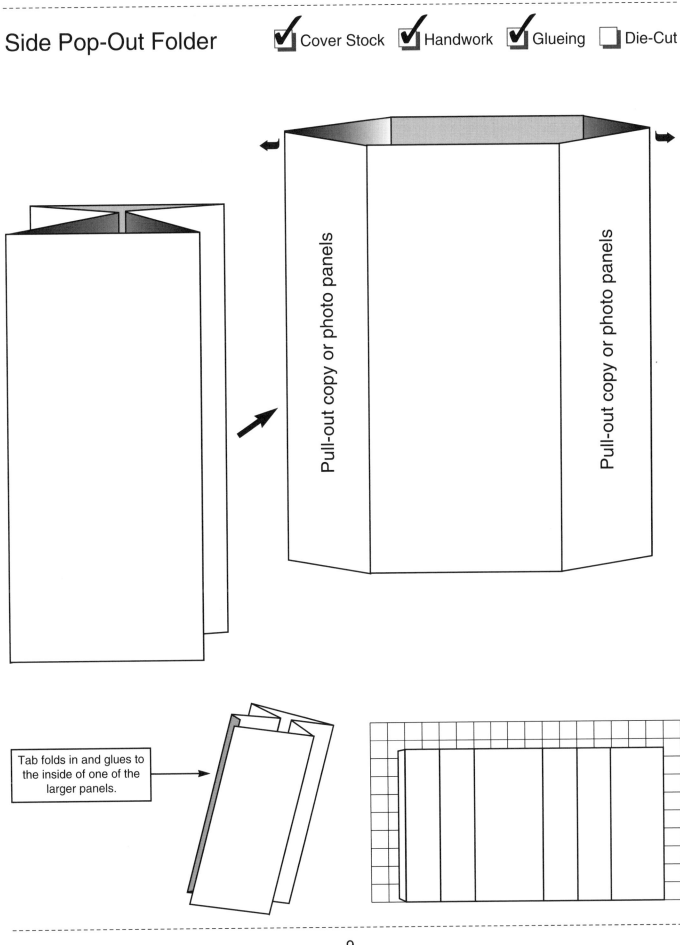

Pull-out copy or photo panels

Pull-out copy or photo panels

Tab folds in and glues to the inside of one of the larger panels.

# Come From Behind Half Cover

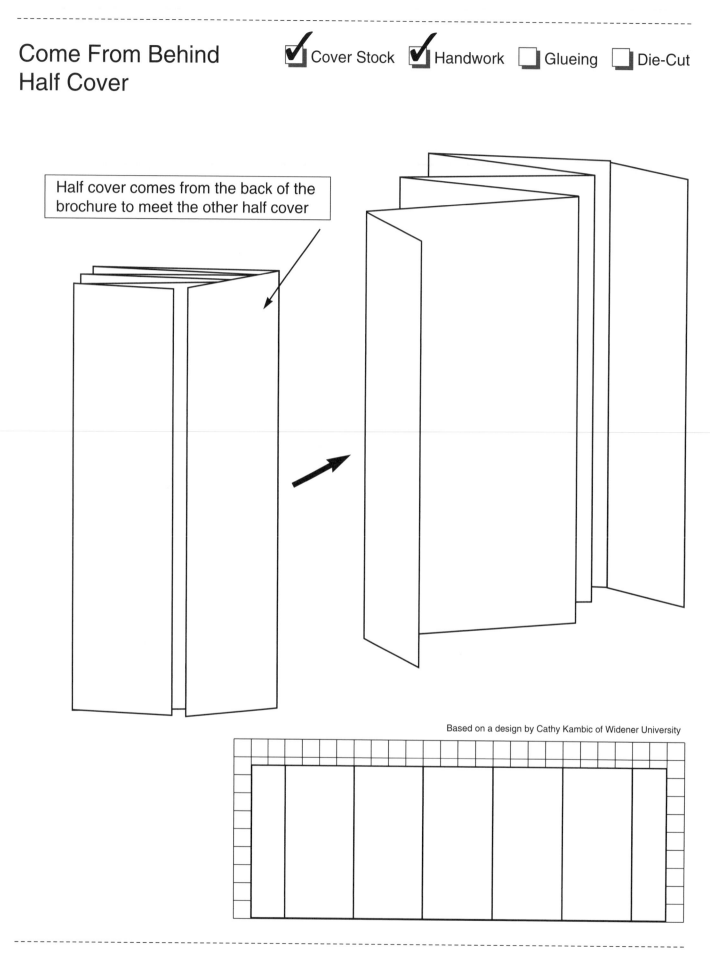

Half cover comes from the back of the brochure to meet the other half cover

Based on a design by Cathy Kambic of Widener University

# Tabbed Booklet

☑ Cover Stock  ☑ Handwork  ☐ Glueing  ☑ Die-Cut

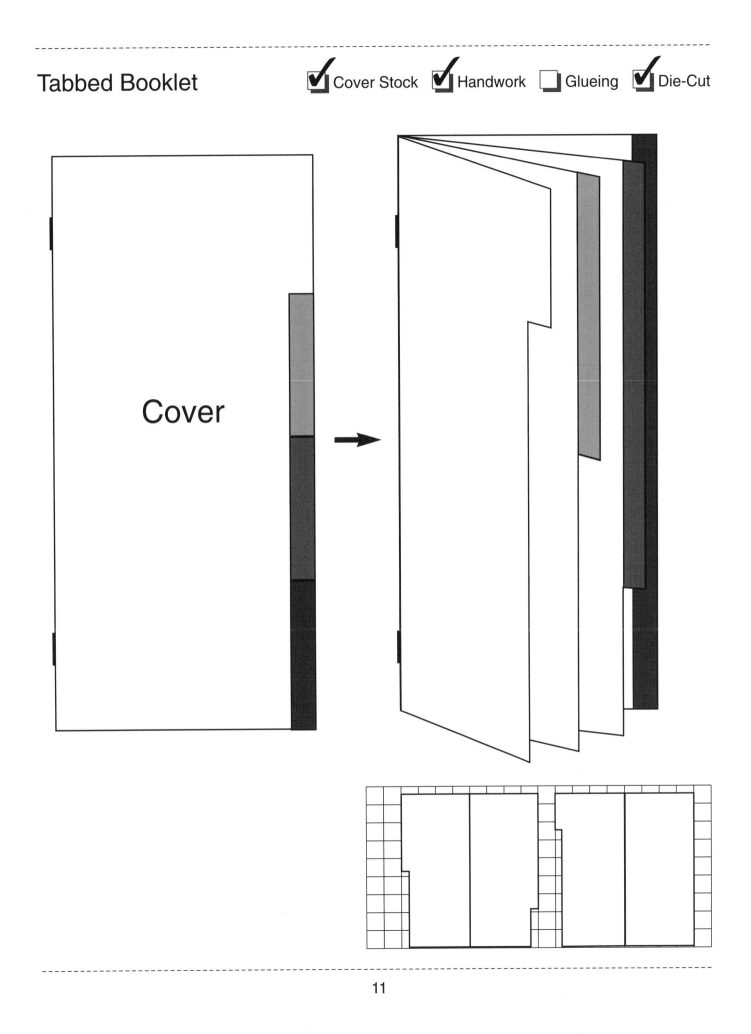

Cover

# Mondrian Fold

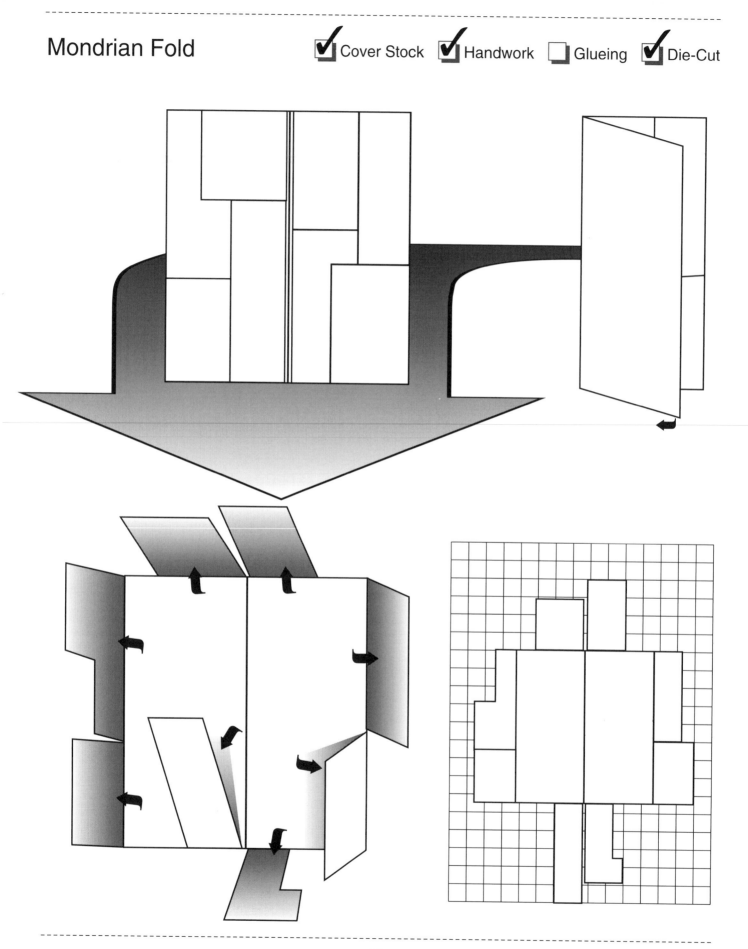

# Table Top Fold Out

This baby packs a lot of information. Should be laid out on a table to be properly displayed Finished size doesn't matter. The top panels are meant to fold out first and then their corresponding lower panels.

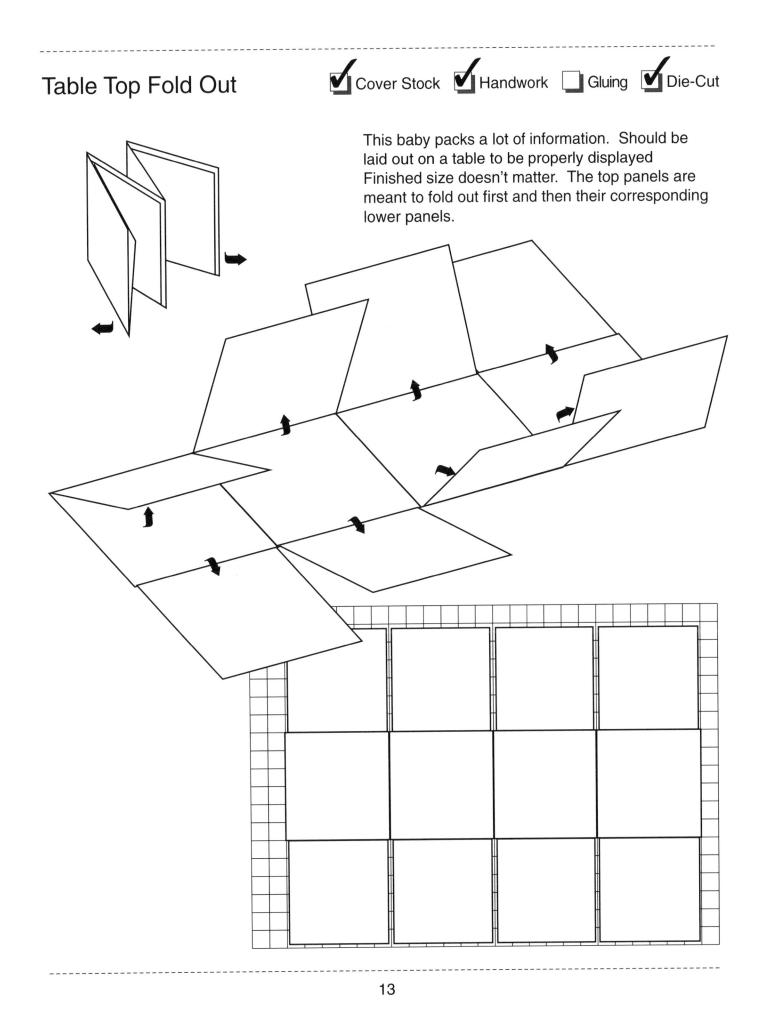

# Folder and Business Card Combo

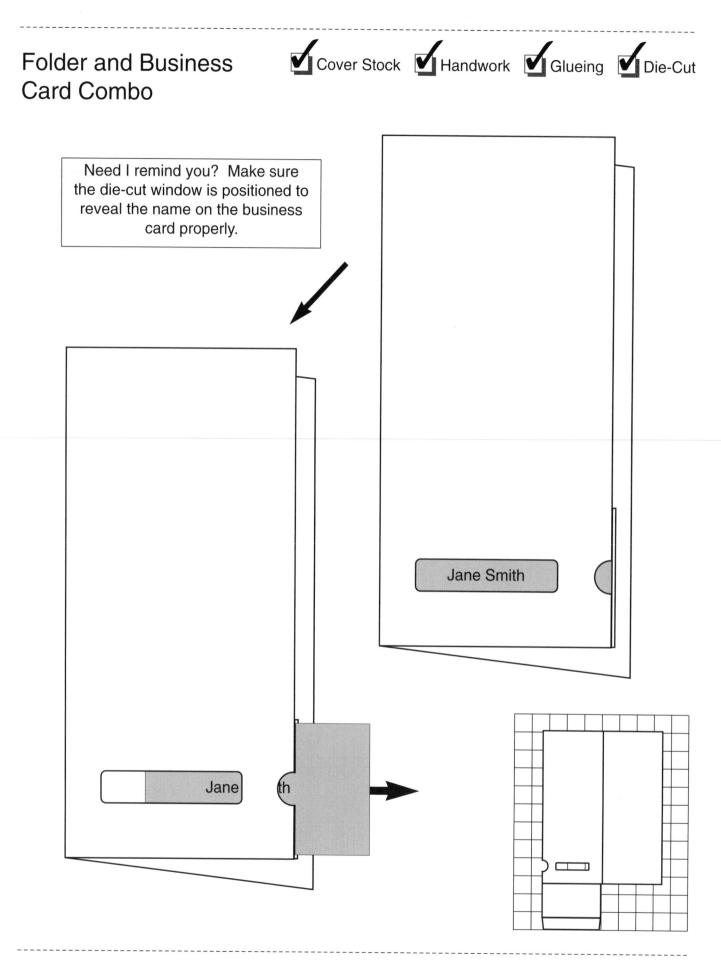

Need I remind you?  Make sure the die-cut window is positioned to reveal the name on the business card properly.

Jane Smith

Jane th

# Windows Folder

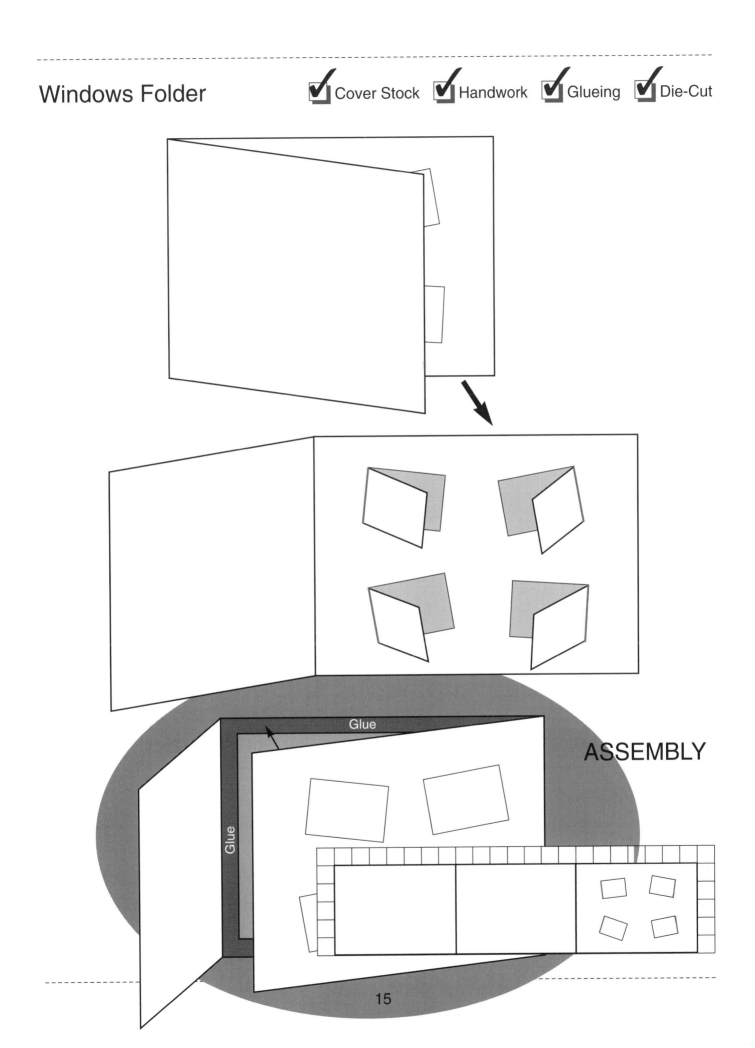

Cover Stock ✓ Handwork ✓ Glueing ✓ Die-Cut ✓

Glue

Glue

ASSEMBLY

# Locking cover folder

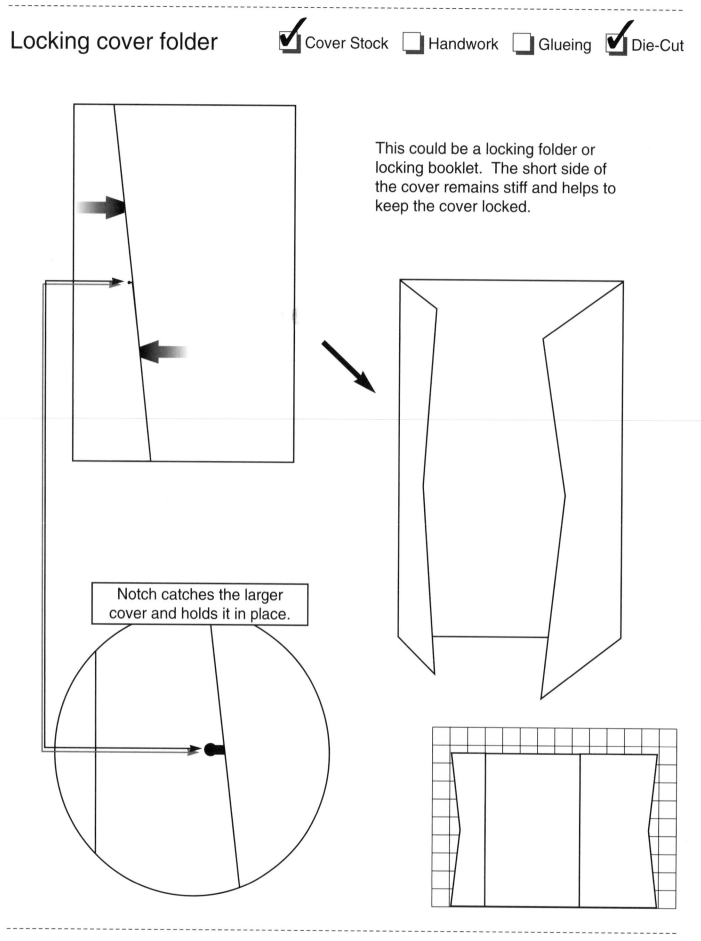

This could be a locking folder or locking booklet. The short side of the cover remains stiff and helps to keep the cover locked.

Notch catches the larger cover and holds it in place.

# Fold-Out Folder

Prints one side. Could be used for a map, too.

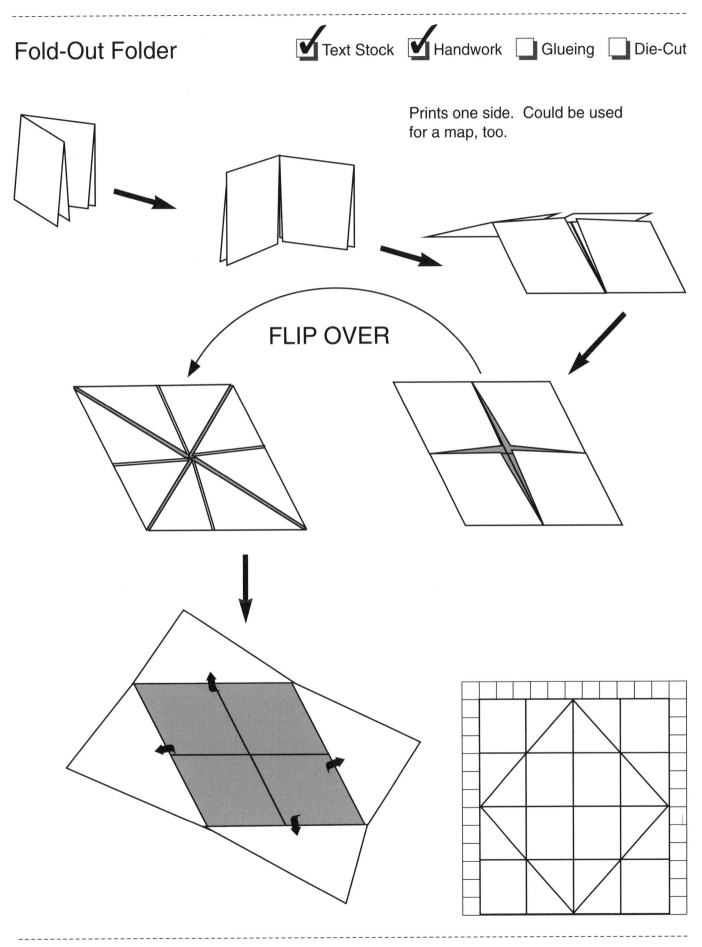

FLIP OVER

# Rolodex/Business Card Folder

☑ Cover Stock  ☐ Handwork  ☐ Glueing  ☑ Die-Cut

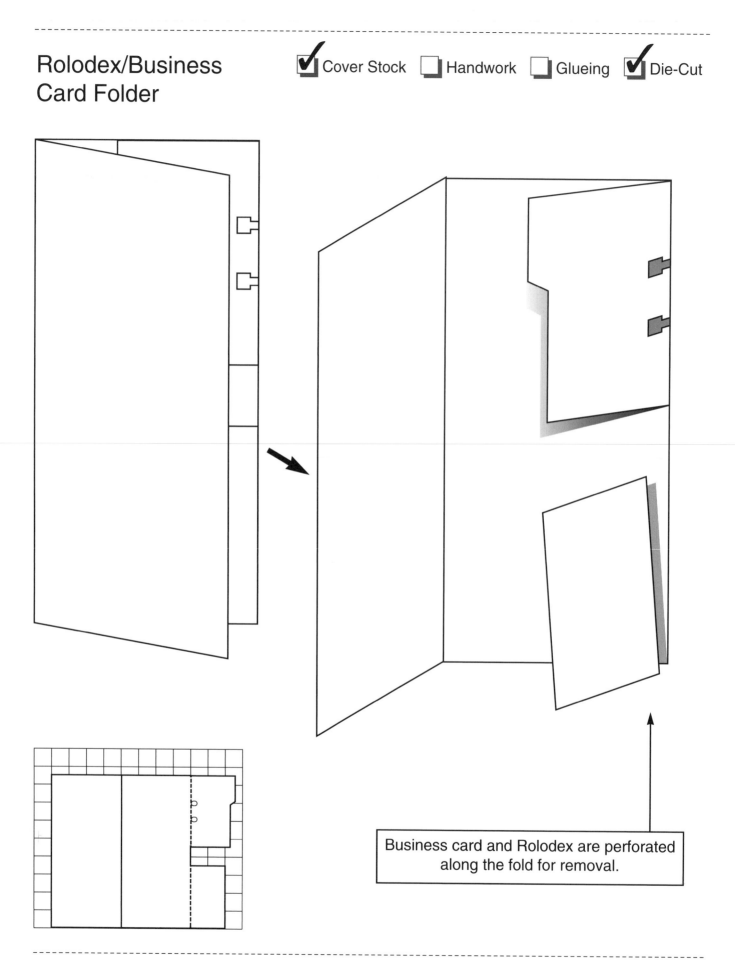

Business card and Rolodex are perforated along the fold for removal.

18

## Soft Fold Booklet

☑ Text Stock ☐ Handwork ☐ Glueing ☐ Die-Cut

Number of pages – your choice. Second fold is a soft fold; no scoring. This folding idea makes a larger folder in a convenient size. The lighter the paper the better.

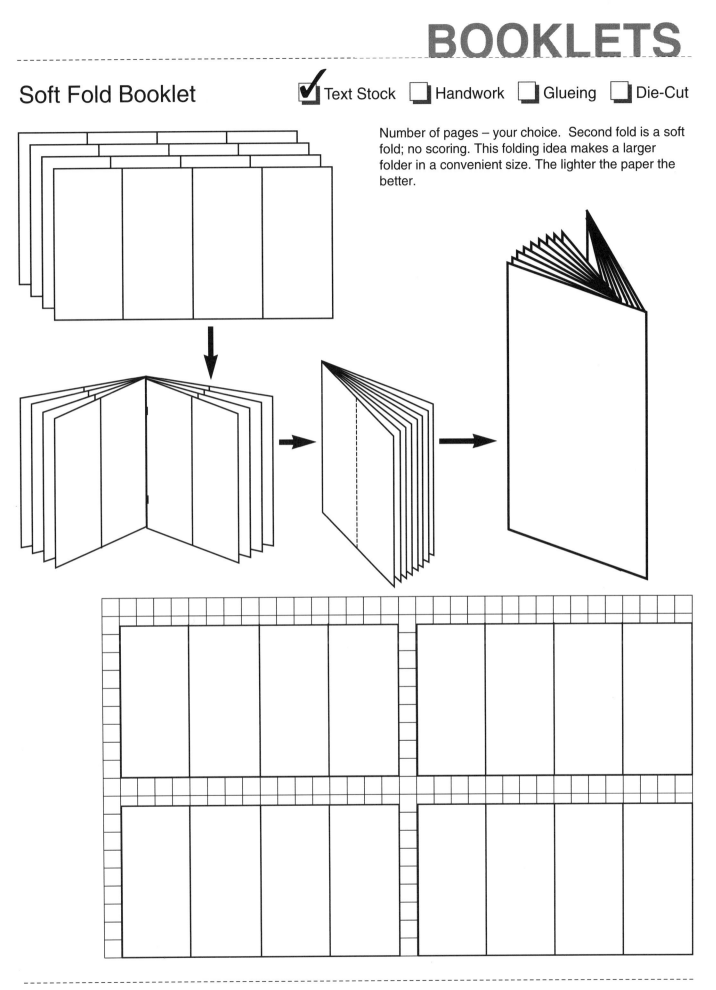

# Booklet Folder

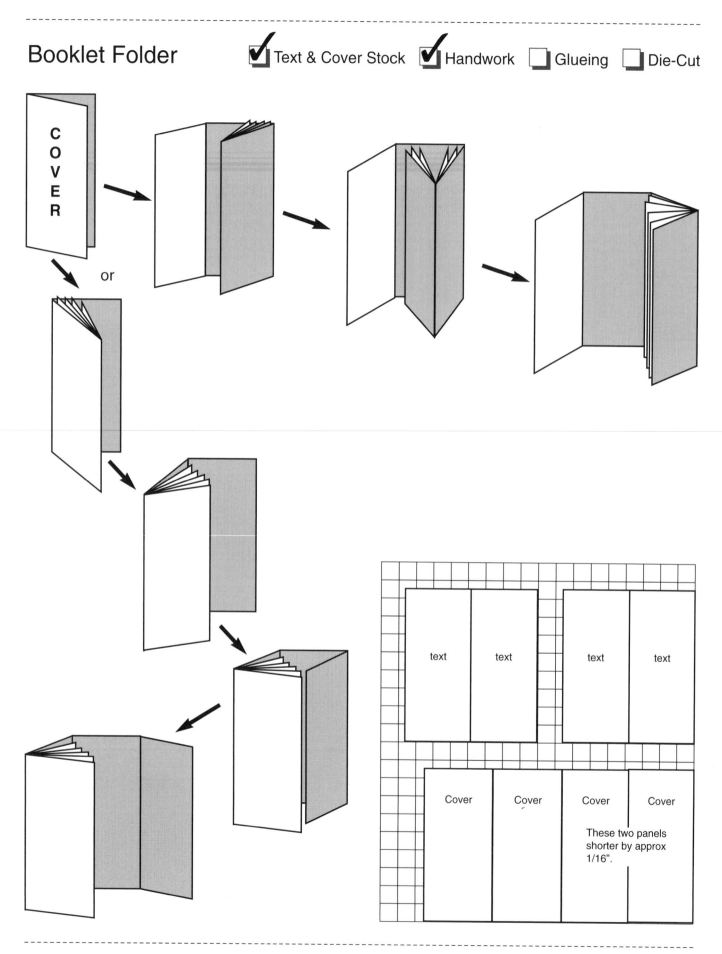

text  text  text  text

Cover  Cover  Cover  Cover

These two panels shorter by approx 1/16".

# Folder Cover on Booklet

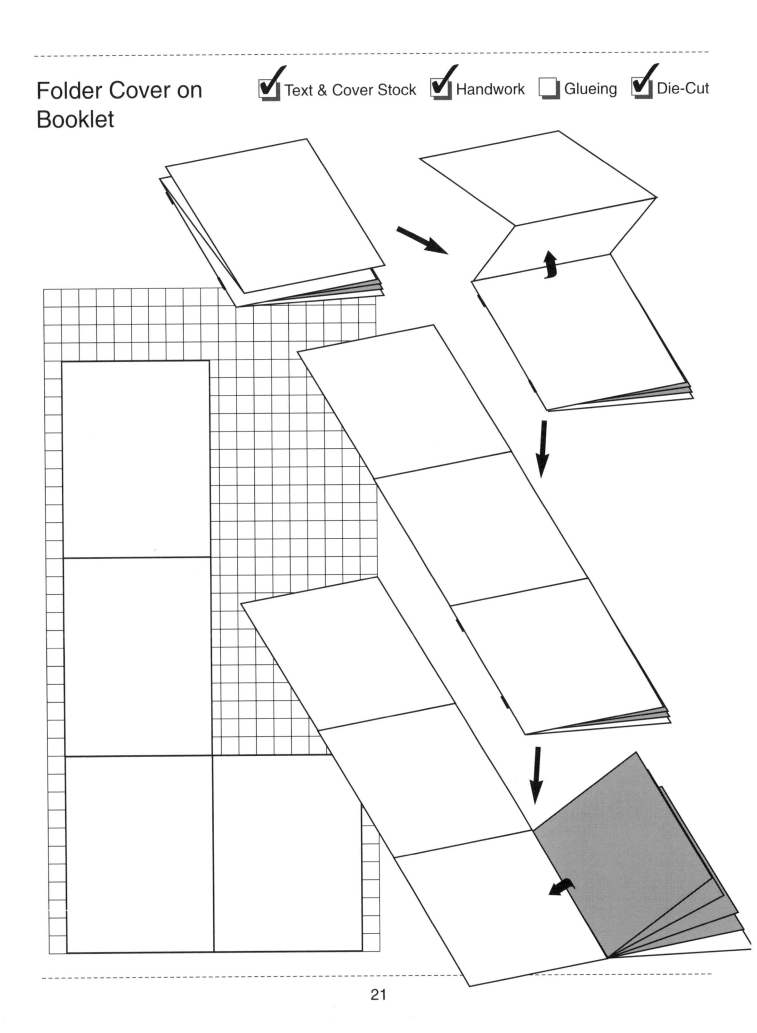

# Booklet with Tiered Pages

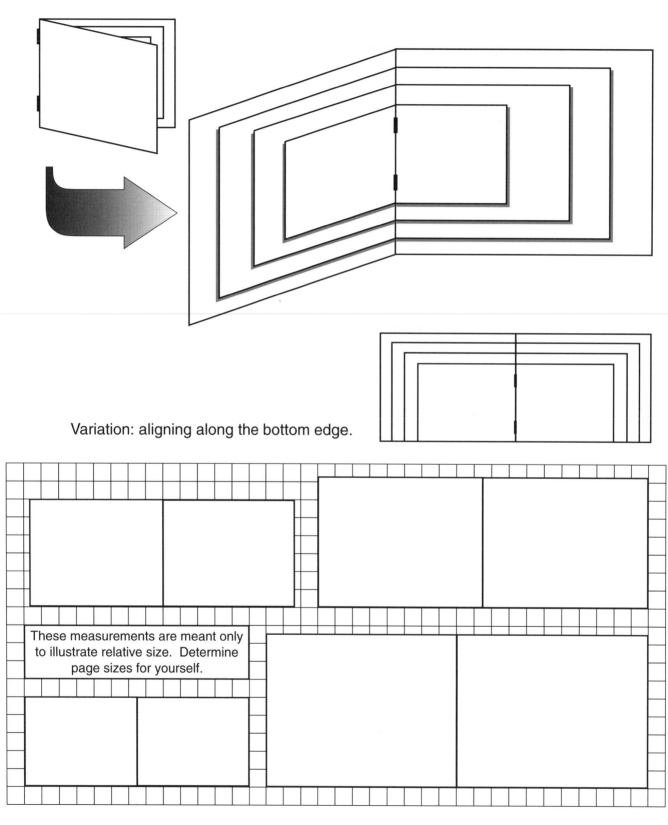

Variation: aligning along the bottom edge.

These measurements are meant only to illustrate relative size. Determine page sizes for yourself.

# Booklet with Foldout Display Panels

☑ Text & Cover Stock  ☑ Handwork  ☐ Glueing  ☑ Die-Cut

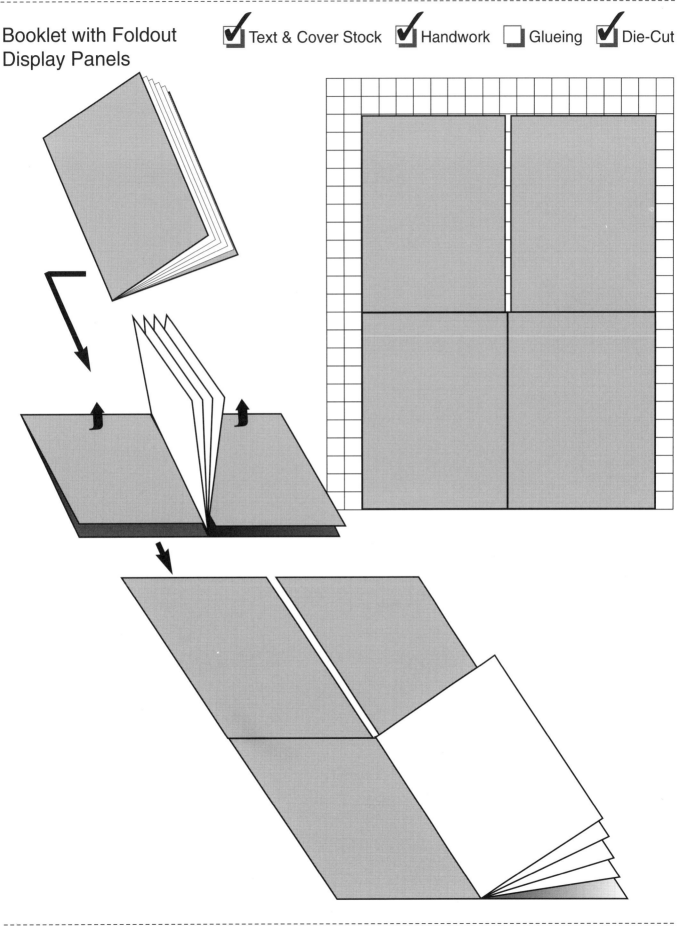

# Front/Back Booklet

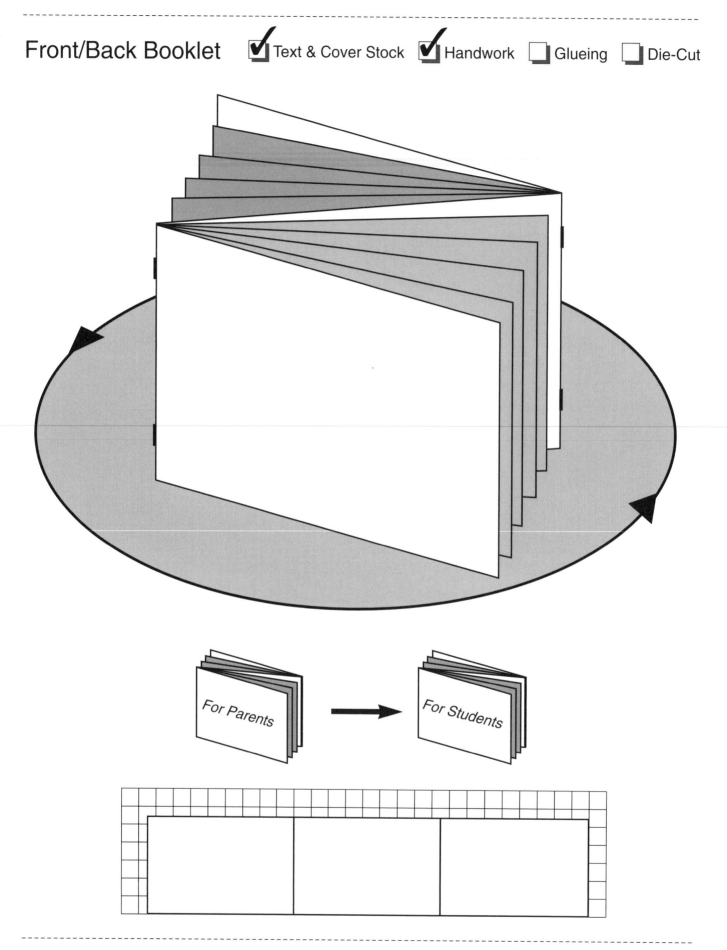

For Parents → For Students

☑ Cover & Text Stock  ☑ Handwork  ☐ Glueing  ☑ Die-Cut

*Your message or graphic here!*

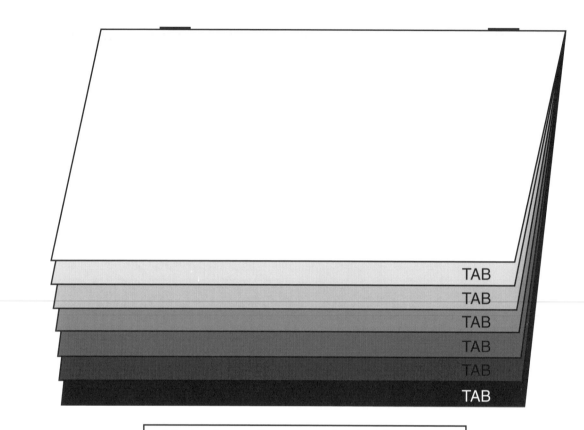

TAB
TAB
TAB
TAB
TAB
TAB

All sheets are the same size but the paper
is folded to different paper widths.

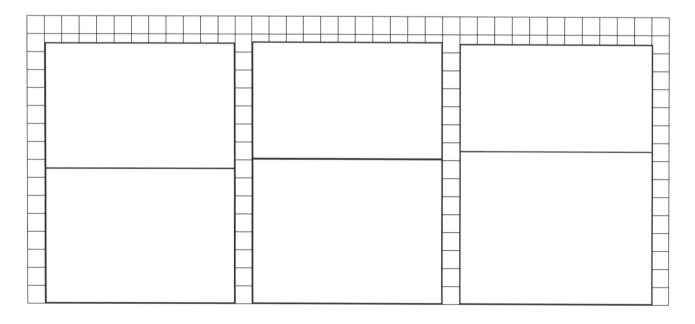

# Stepped pages booklet

The first three pages are stepped. The last three pages are full size.

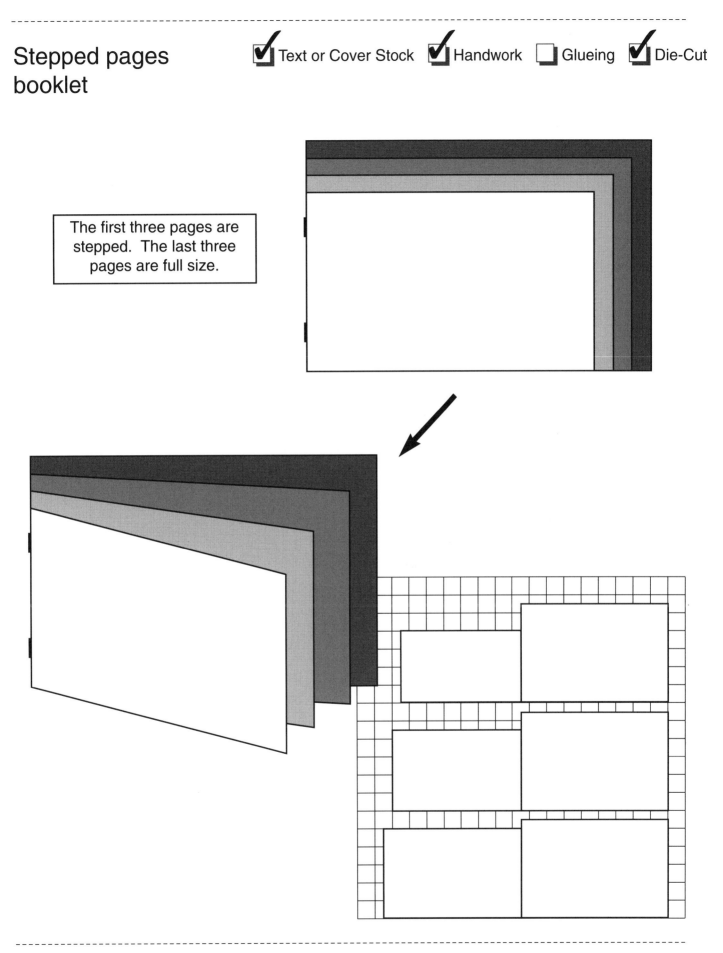

# Long/Short Booklet

☑ Text & Cover Stock ☑ Handwork ☐ Glueing ☐ Die-Cut

Every spread is a full size page and a short page. These pages are then stapled together.

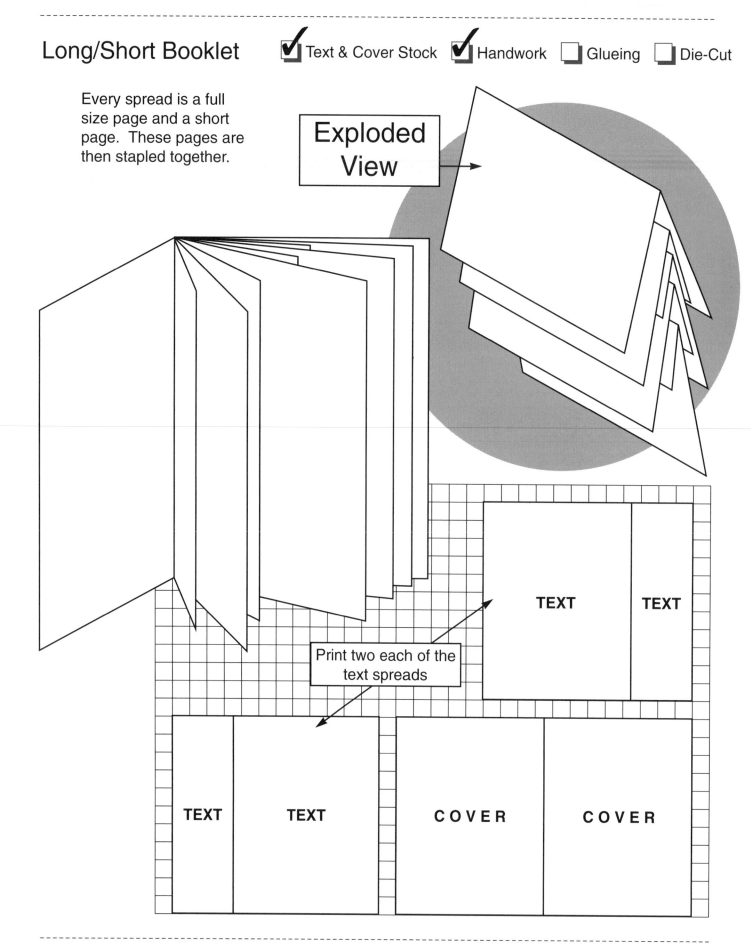

Exploded View

Print two each of the text spreads

TEXT TEXT

TEXT TEXT

COVER COVER

# Mix n' Match Booklet ✔ Text or Cover Stock ✔ Handwork ☐ Glueing ✔ Die-Cut

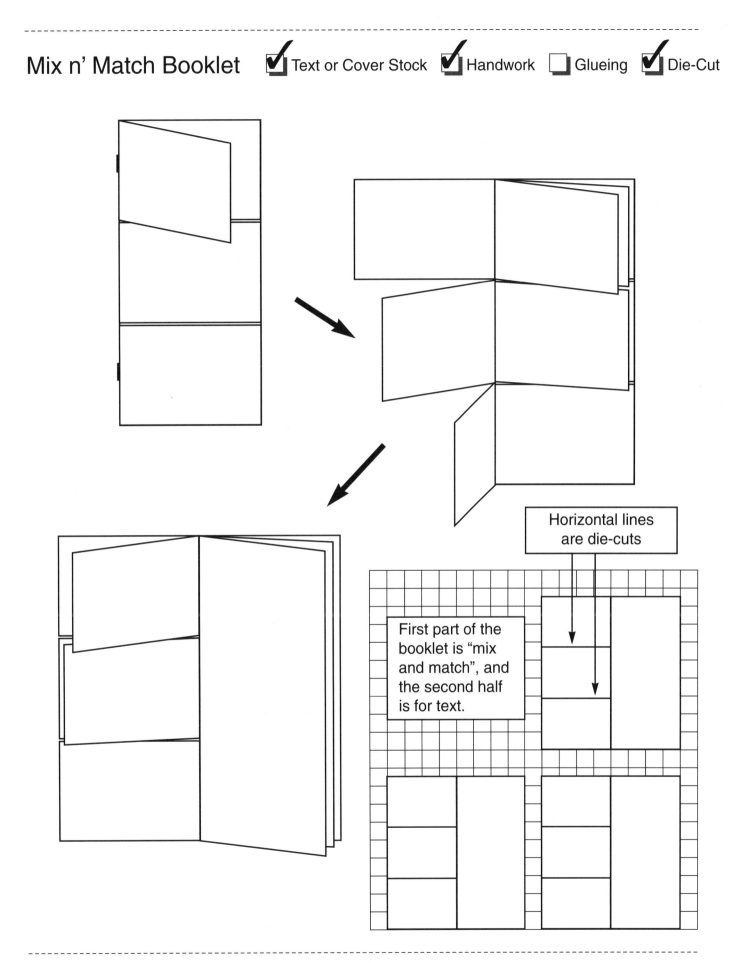

Horizontal lines are die-cuts

First part of the booklet is "mix and match", and the second half is for text.

# Rhomboid Booklet

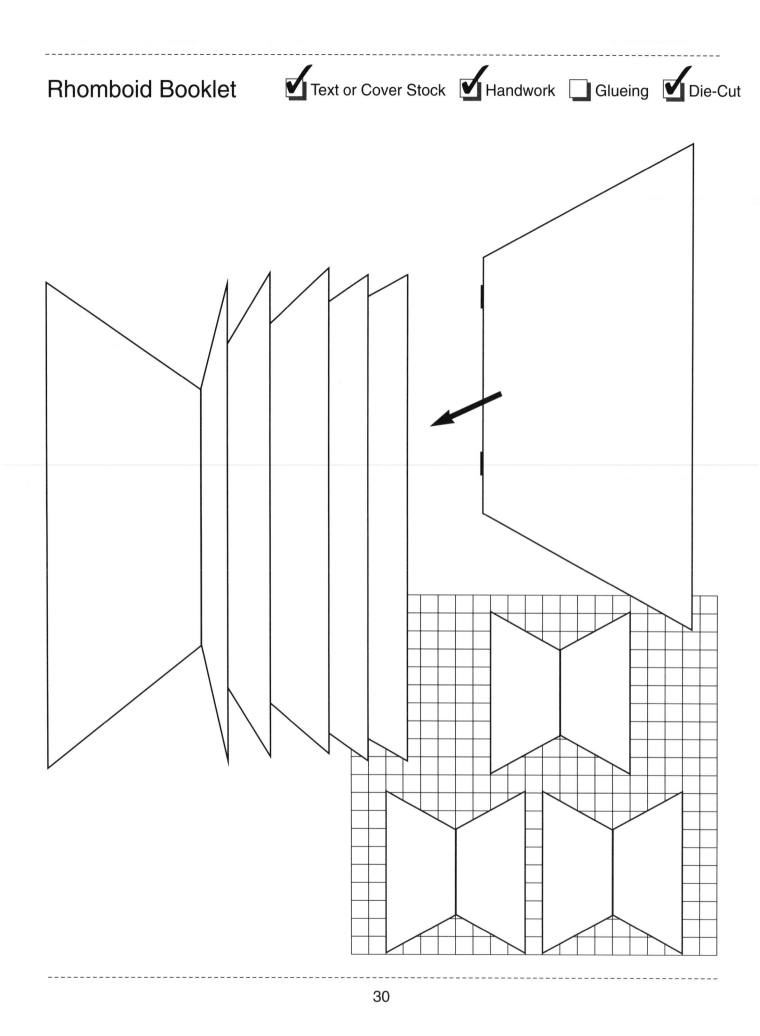

# Booklet with Page Pocket ☑ Text &Cover Stock ☑ Handwork ☑ Glueing ☑ Die-Cut

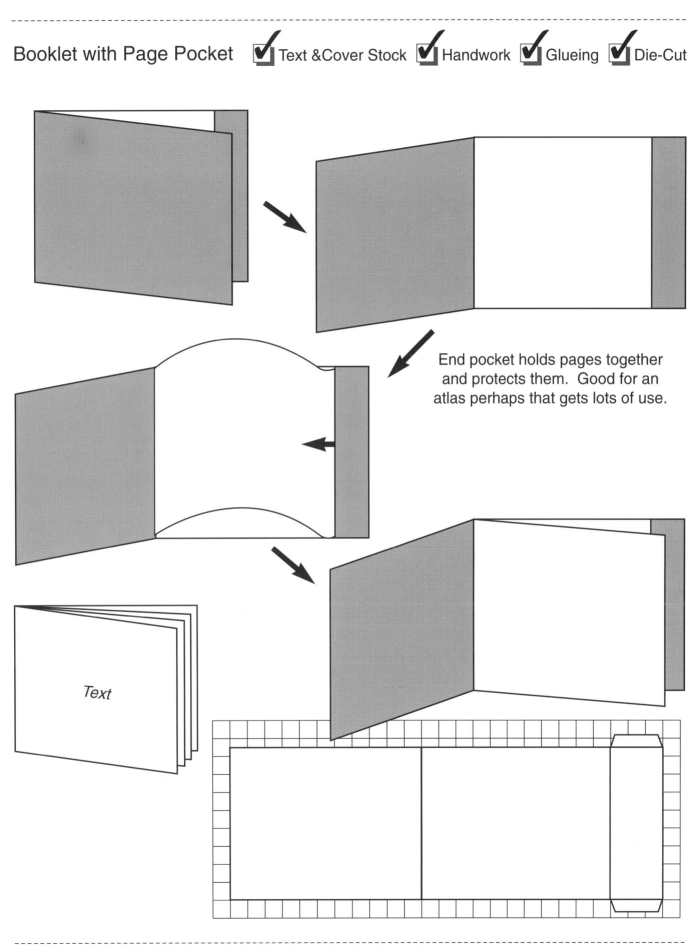

End pocket holds pages together and protects them. Good for an atlas perhaps that gets lots of use.

Text

# 3 Booklet Booklet

☑ Text & Cover Stock  ☑ Handwork  ☐ Glueing  ☐ Die-Cut

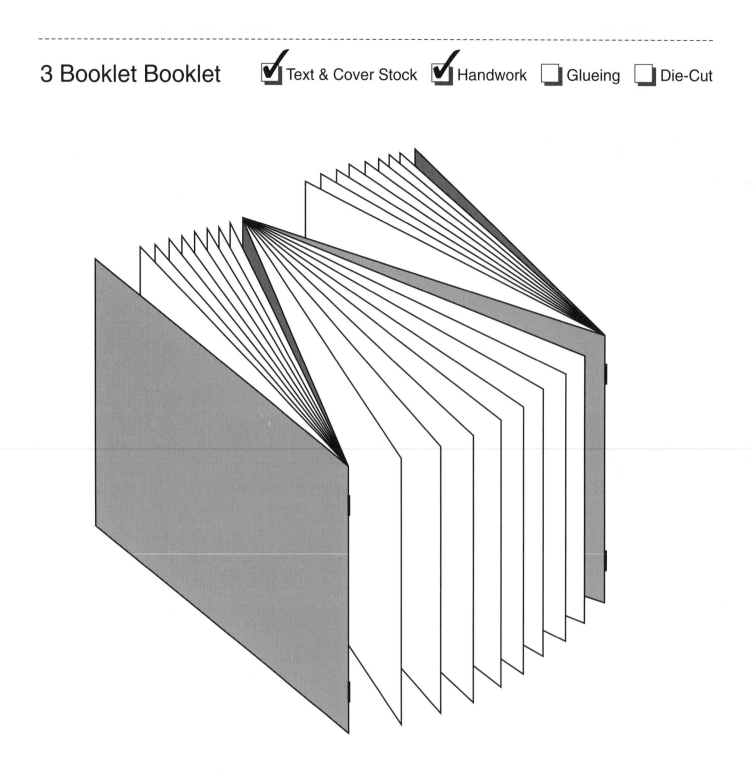

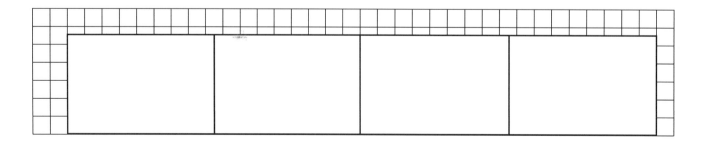

# Booklet with Concealed Binding

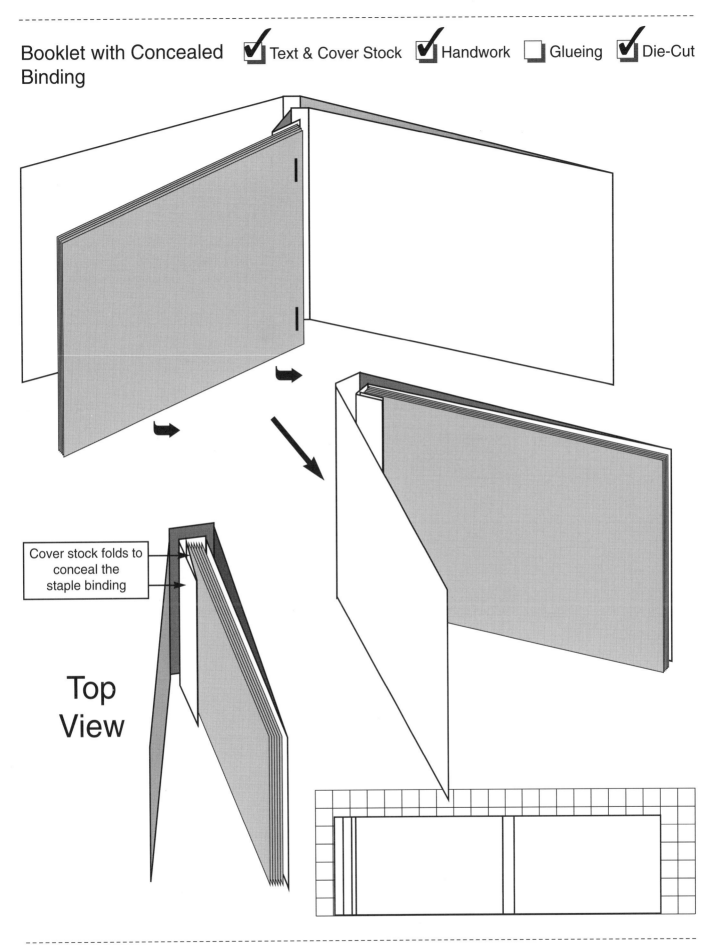

Cover stock folds to conceal the staple binding

Top View

# Irregular Page Booklet

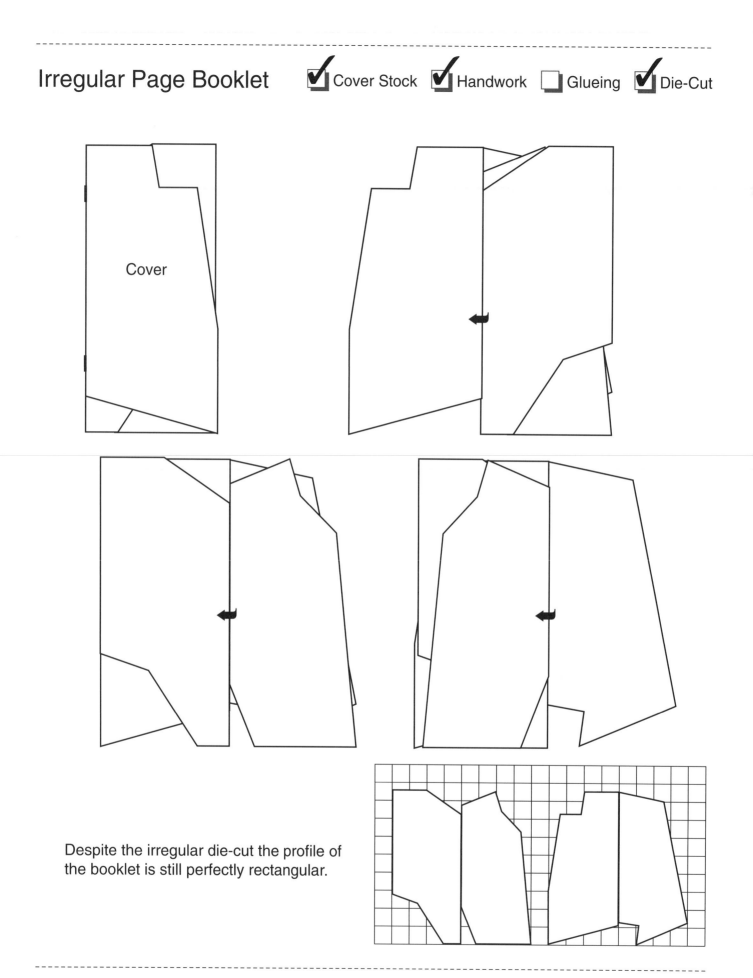

Cover

Despite the irregular die-cut the profile of
the booklet is still perfectly rectangular.

# POCKET FOLDERS

## Full Pocket/Half Pocket
## Pocket Folder

☑ Cover Stock  ☑ Handwork  ☑ Glueing  ☑ Die-Cut

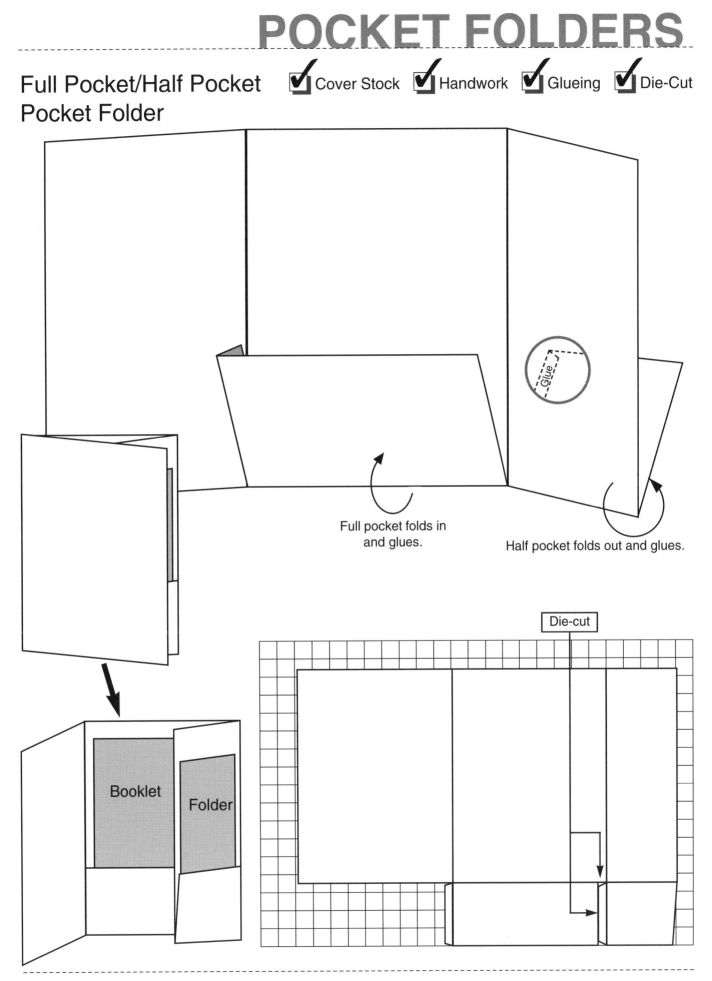

Full pocket folds in and glues.

Half pocket folds out and glues.

Glue

Booklet    Folder

Die-cut

# Folder with Locking Device
☑ Cover Stock  ☑ Handwork  ☐ Glueing  ☑ Die-Cut

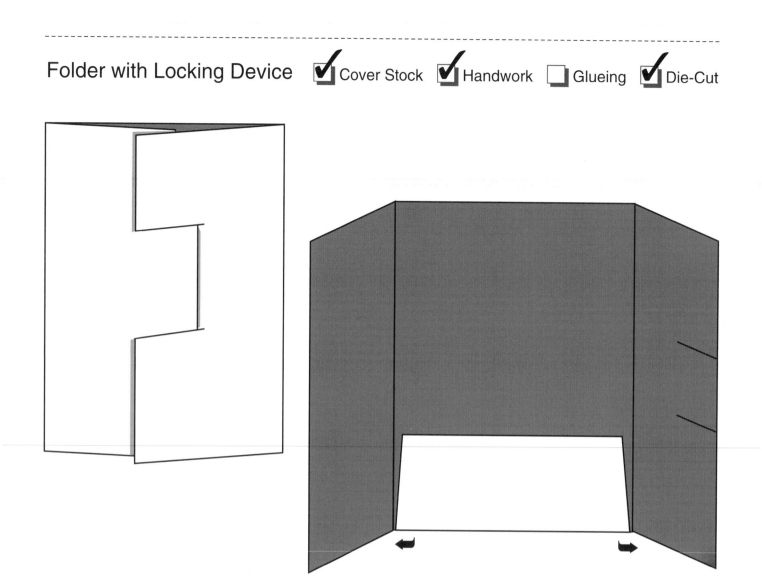

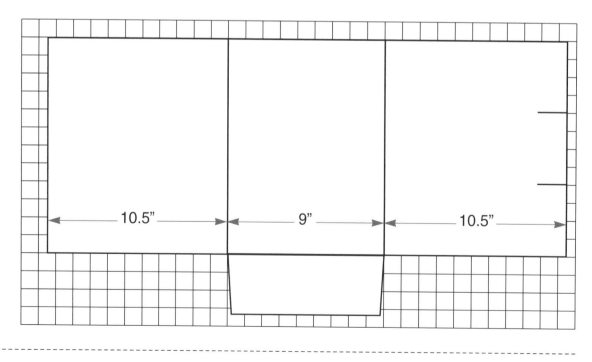

10.5"    9"    10.5"

# Folder Folder Holder

☑ Text or Cover Stock ☑ Handwork ☐ Glueing ☐ Die-Cut

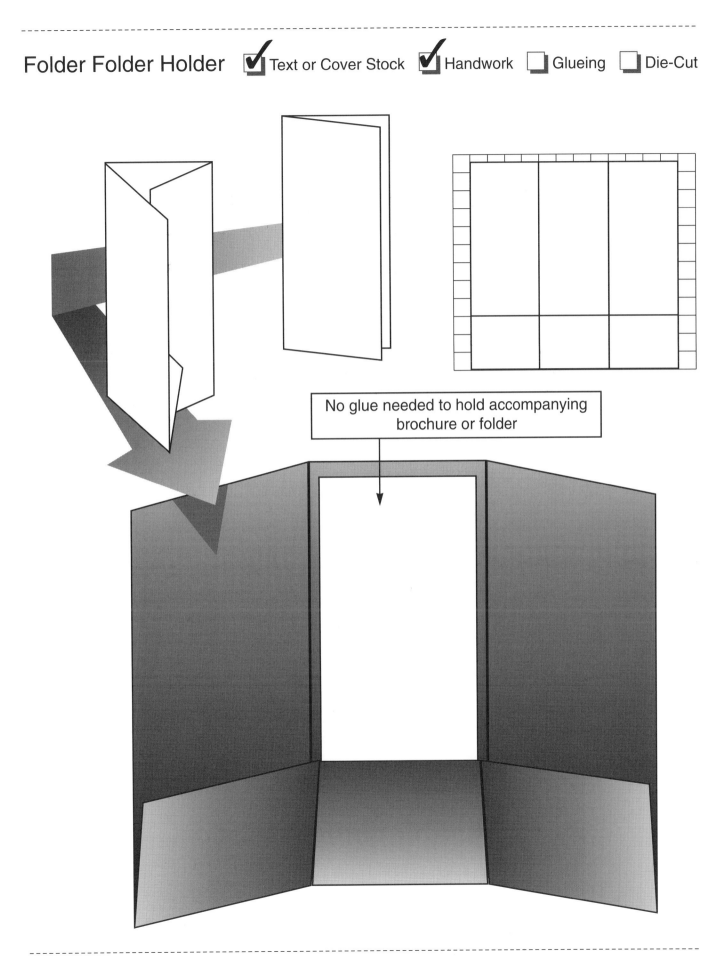

No glue needed to hold accompanying brochure or folder

# Folder with Envelop Slot

Slit width of a busi-
ness envelop

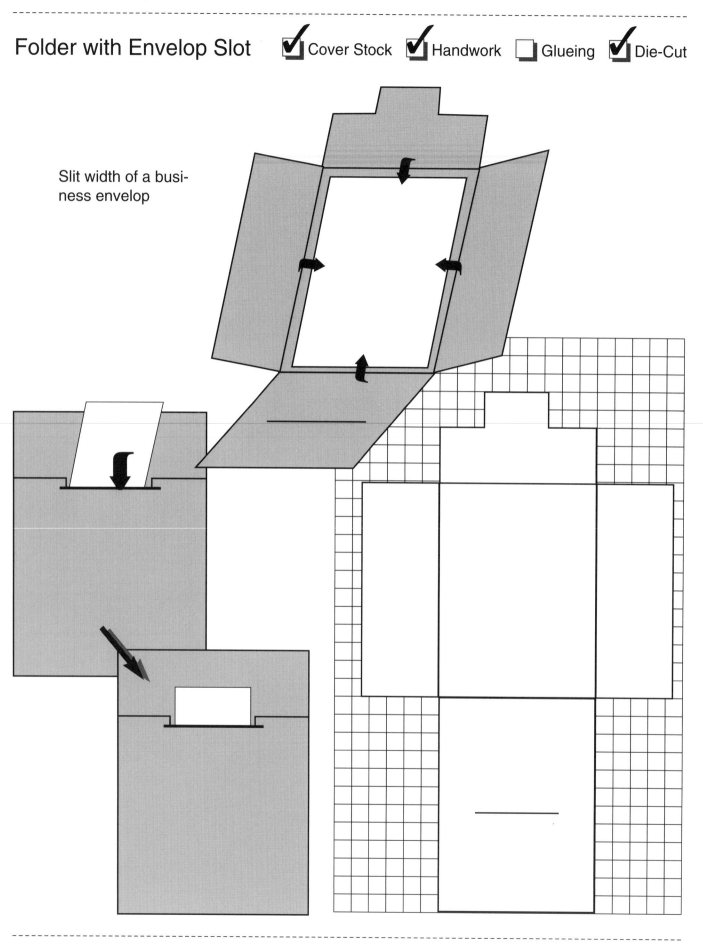

# Bill Fold

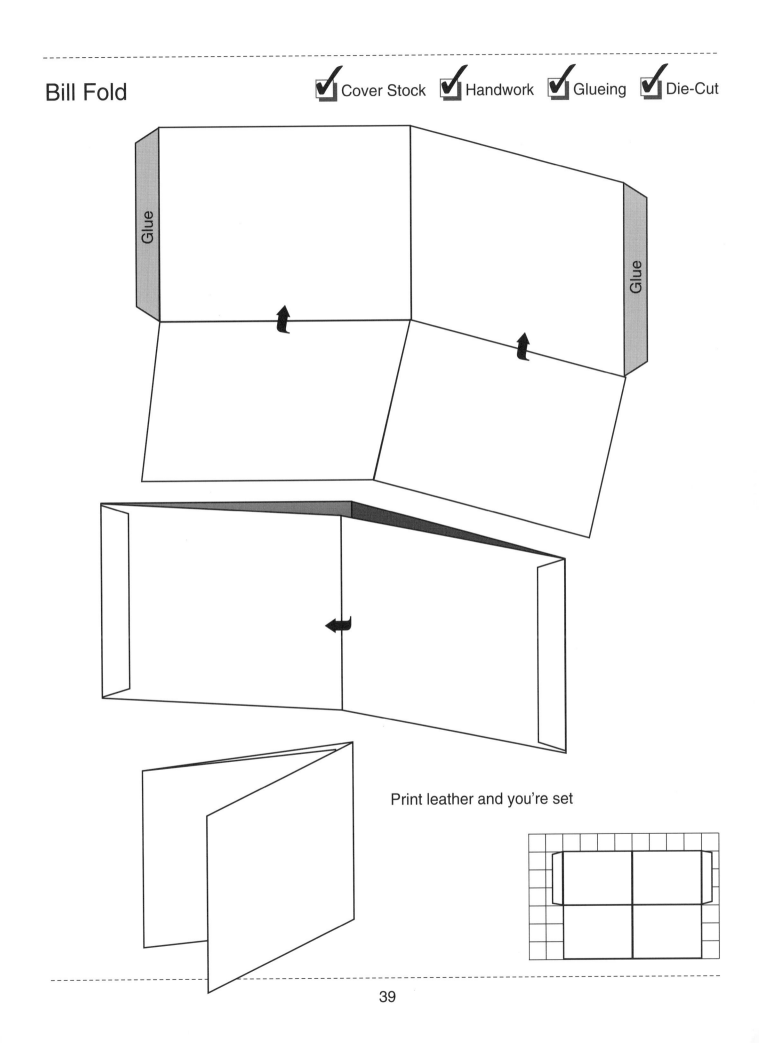

Glue

Glue

Print leather and you're set

# Double-Pocket Pocket Folder

Cover Stock ✓ Handwork ✓ Glueing ✓ Die-Cut ✓

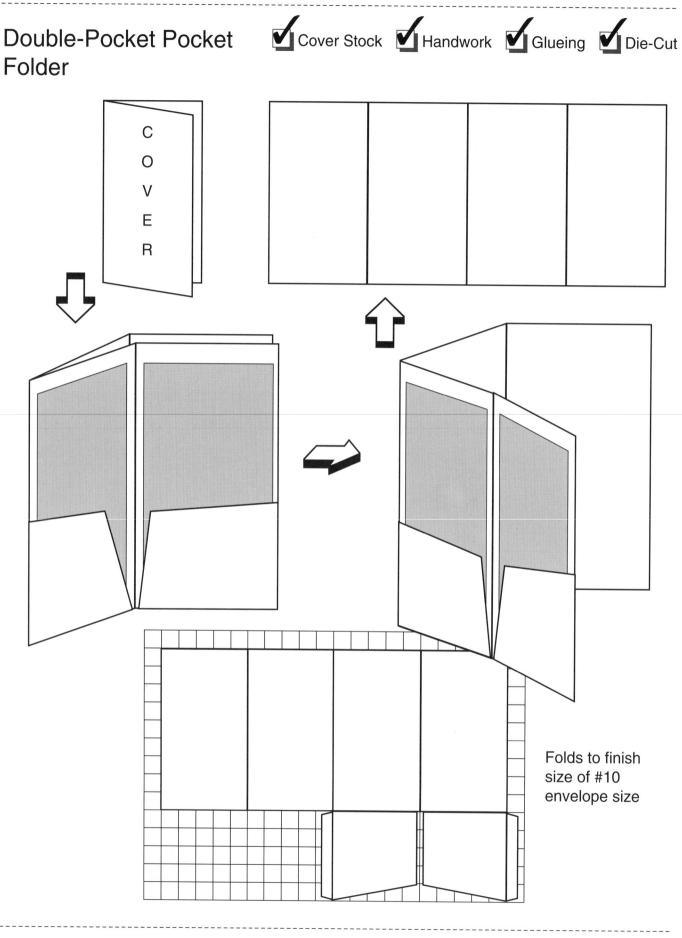

Folds to finish size of #10 envelope size

# "Free Standing Pocket"

☑ Text Cover Stock ☑ Handwork ☑ Glueing ☑ Die-Cut

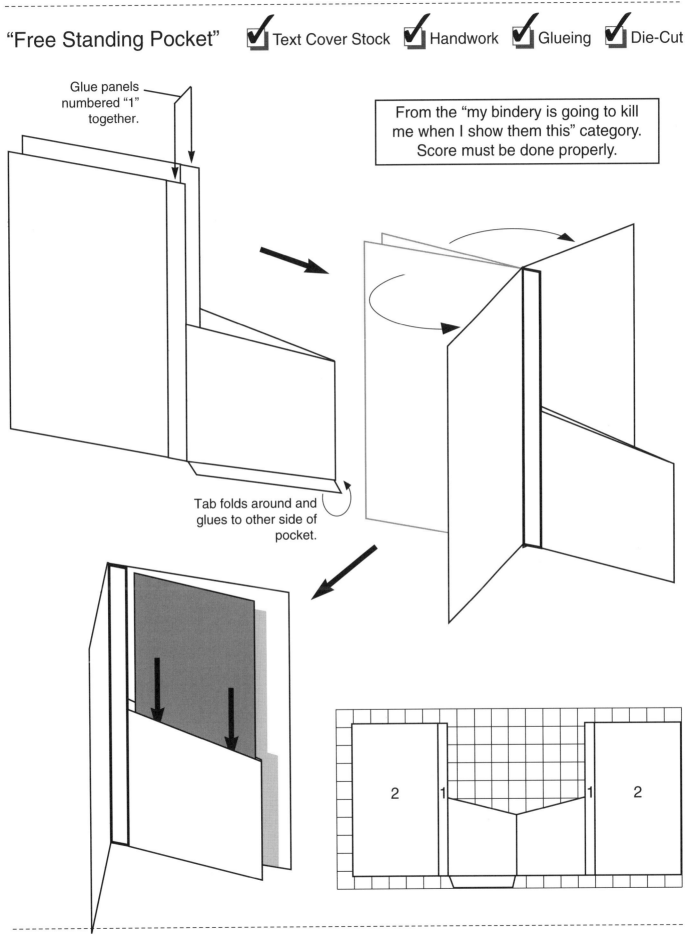

Glue panels numbered "1" together.

From the "my bindery is going to kill me when I show them this" category. Score must be done properly.

Tab folds around and glues to other side of pocket.

2 | 1 | 1 | 2

# Brochure Portfolio

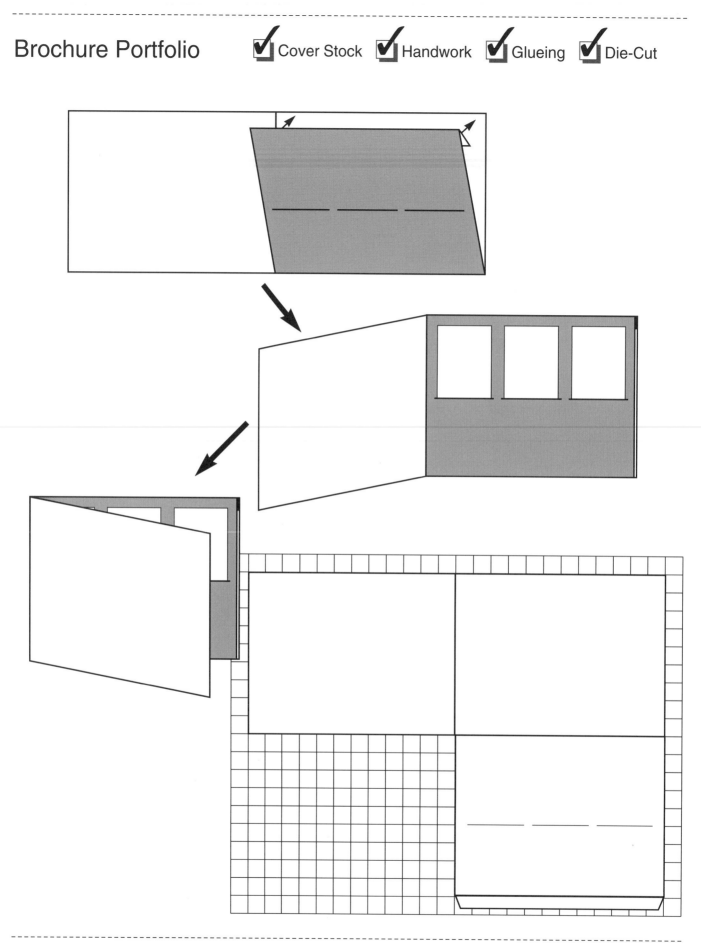

# Folder and Booklet

☑ Text & Cover Stock  ☑ Handwork  ☑ Glueing  ☑ Die-Cut

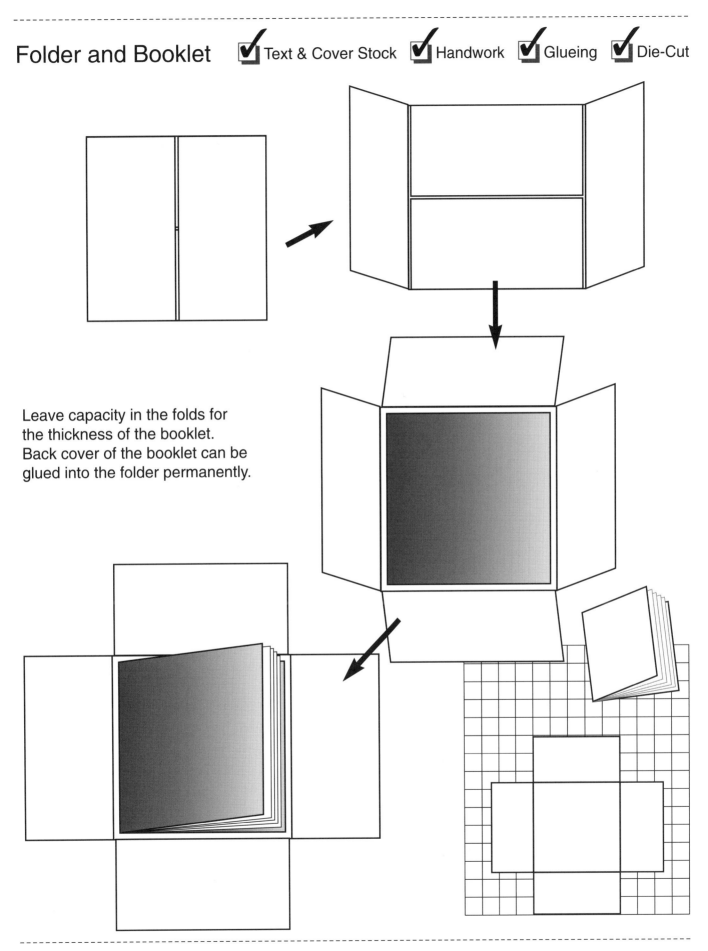

Leave capacity in the folds for the thickness of the booklet. Back cover of the booklet can be glued into the folder permanently.

# File Folder

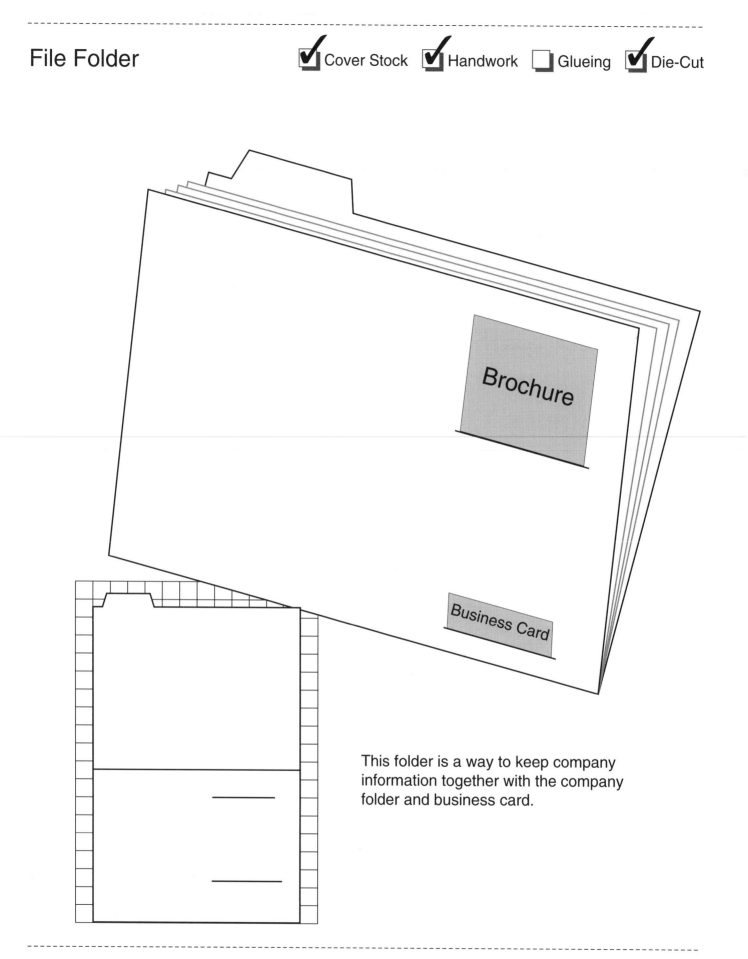

Brochure

Business Card

This folder is a way to keep company information together with the company folder and business card.

# Pocket Folder

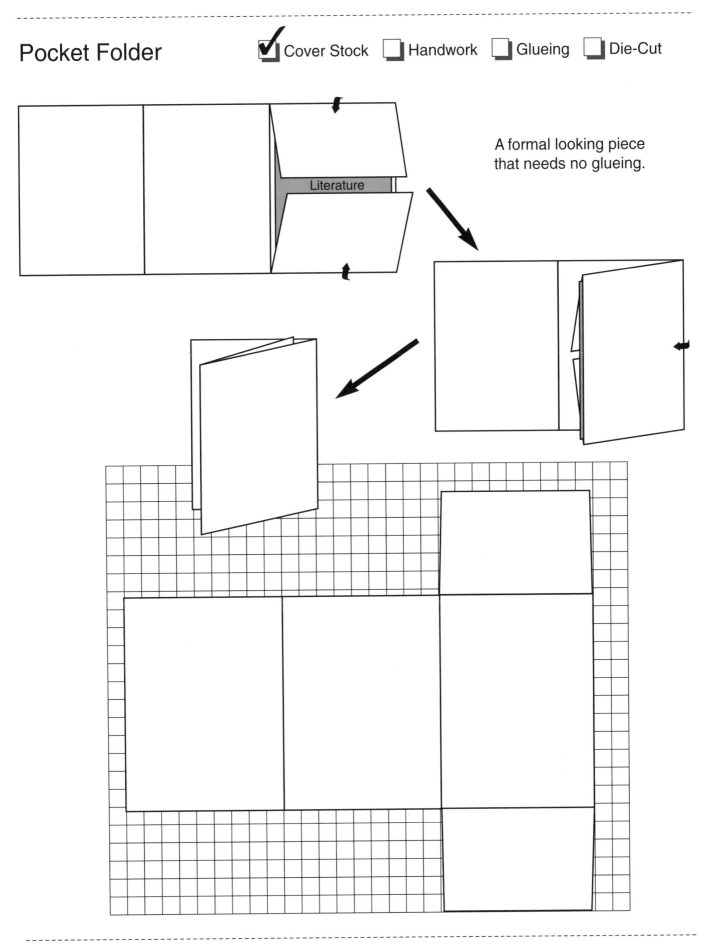

Literature

A formal looking piece that needs no glueing.

# Pocket Folder with Pad ☑Text & Cover Stock ☑Handwork ☑Glueing ☑Die-Cut

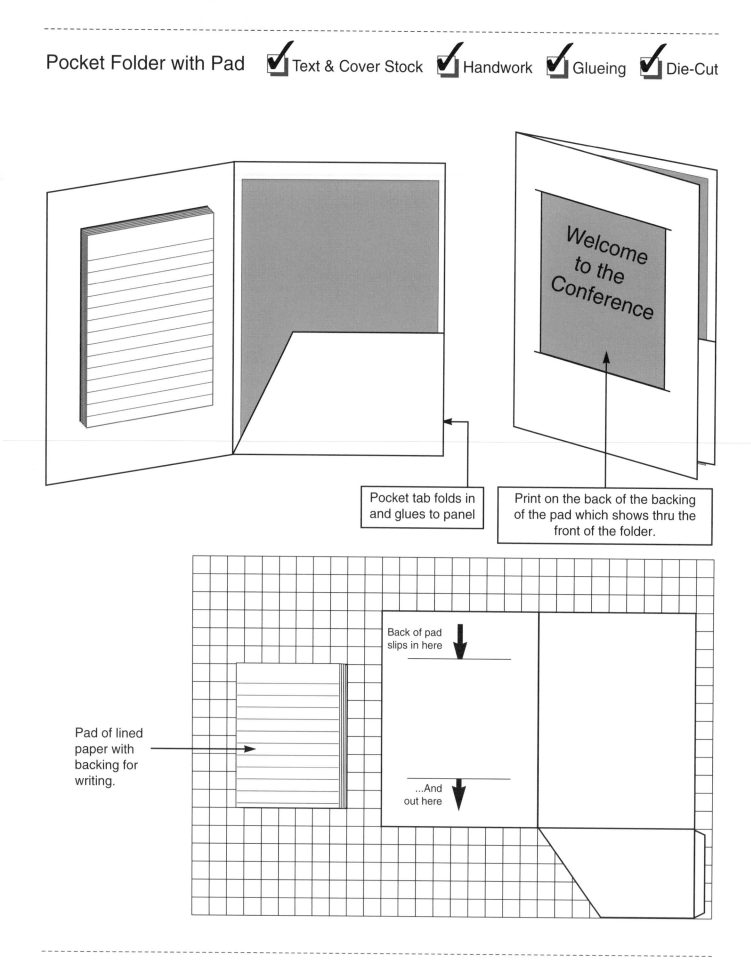

Welcome to the Conference

Pocket tab folds in and glues to panel

Print on the back of the backing of the pad which shows thru the front of the folder.

Back of pad slips in here

Pad of lined paper with backing for writing.

...And out here

# Three Pocket Folder Holder

☑ Cover Stock  ☑ Handwork  ☑ Glueing  ☑ Die-Cut

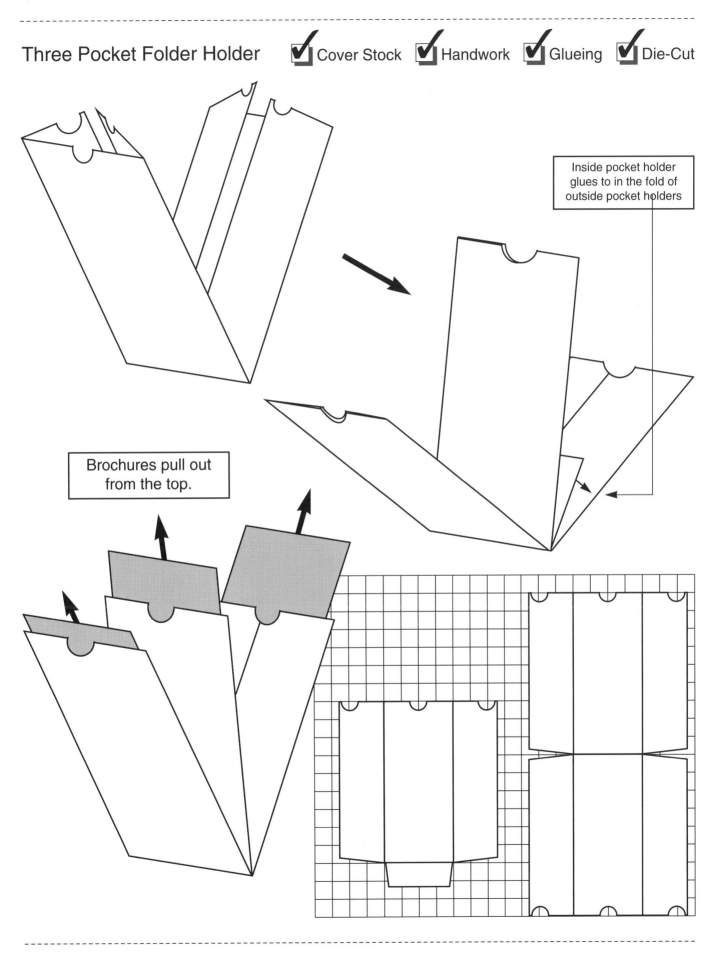

Inside pocket holder glues to in the fold of outside pocket holders

Brochures pull out from the top.

☑ Cover Stock  ☑ Handwork  ☑ Glueing  ☑ Die-Cut

Folds turn in and glue to oppposite panel. Folders can be pulled out of either side.

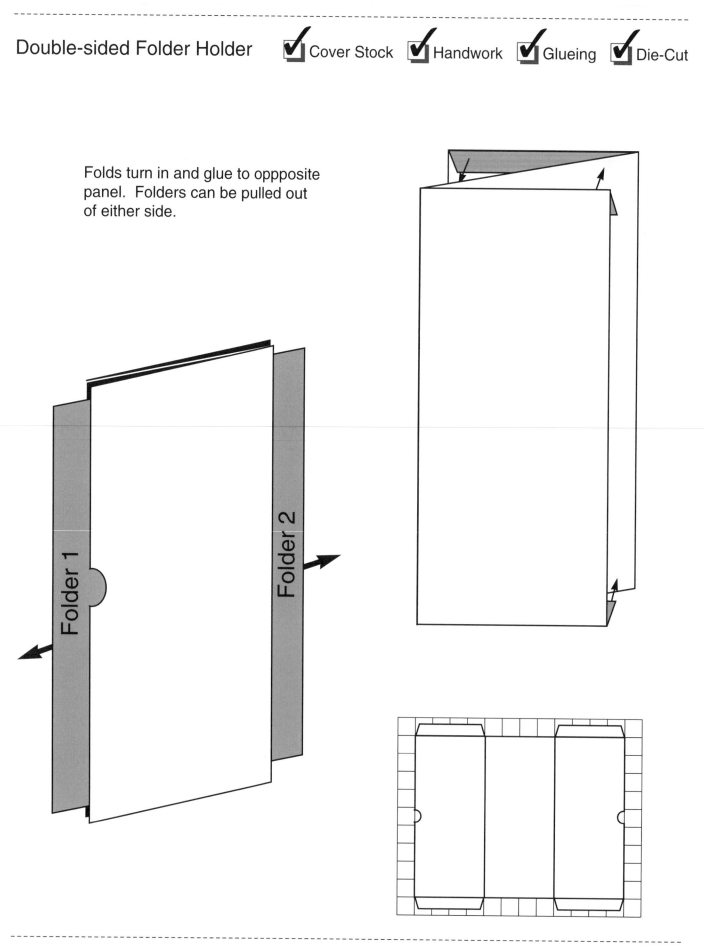

Folder 1

Folder 2

Swing-Out Folder Holder ☑ Text Cover Stock ☑ Handwork ☑ Glueing ☑ Die-Cut

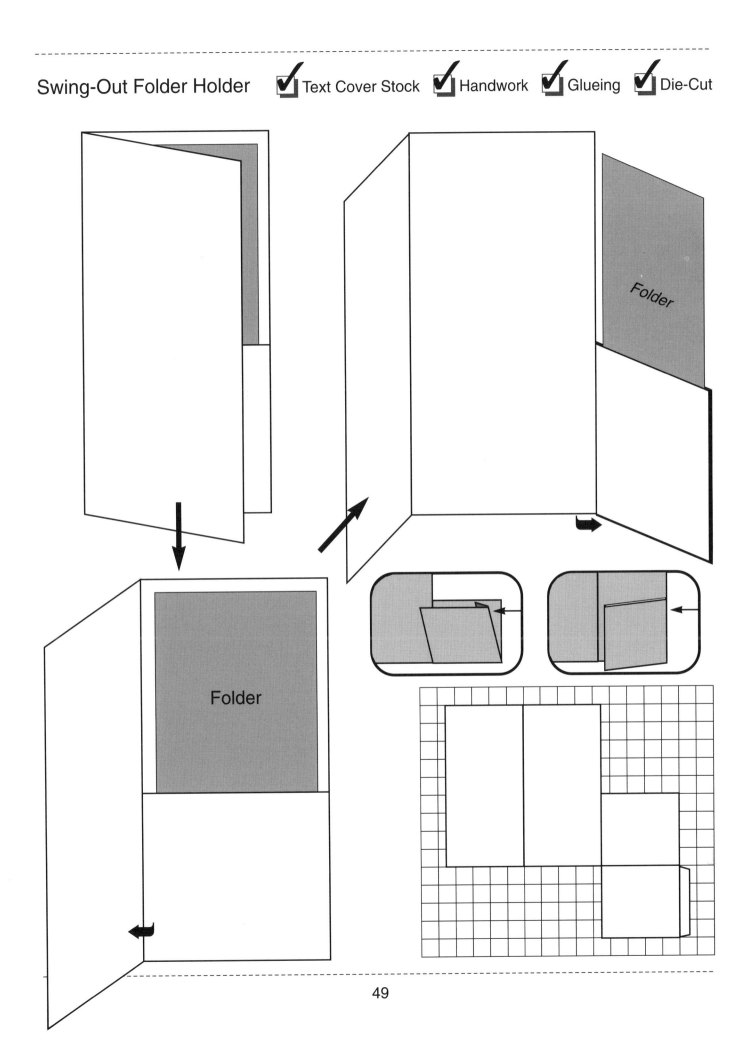

Folder

Folder

# Folio

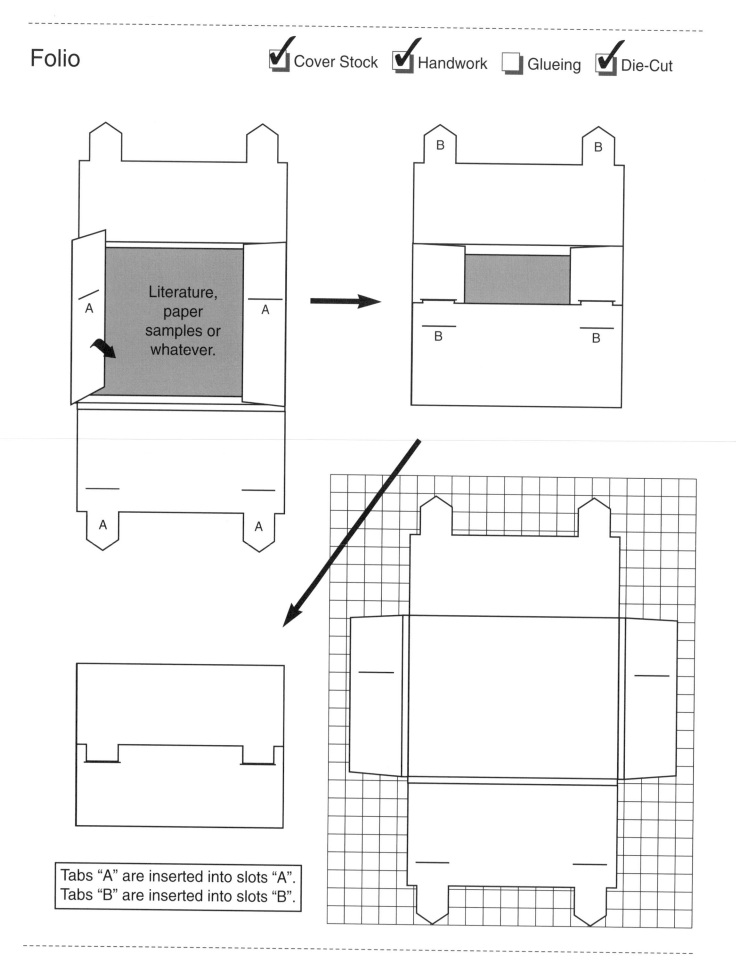

Literature, paper samples or whatever.

A A B B A A B B

Tabs "A" are inserted into slots "A".
Tabs "B" are inserted into slots "B".

# Tiered Folder Holder

☑ Cover Stock  ☑ Handwork  ☑ Glueing  ☑ Die-Cut

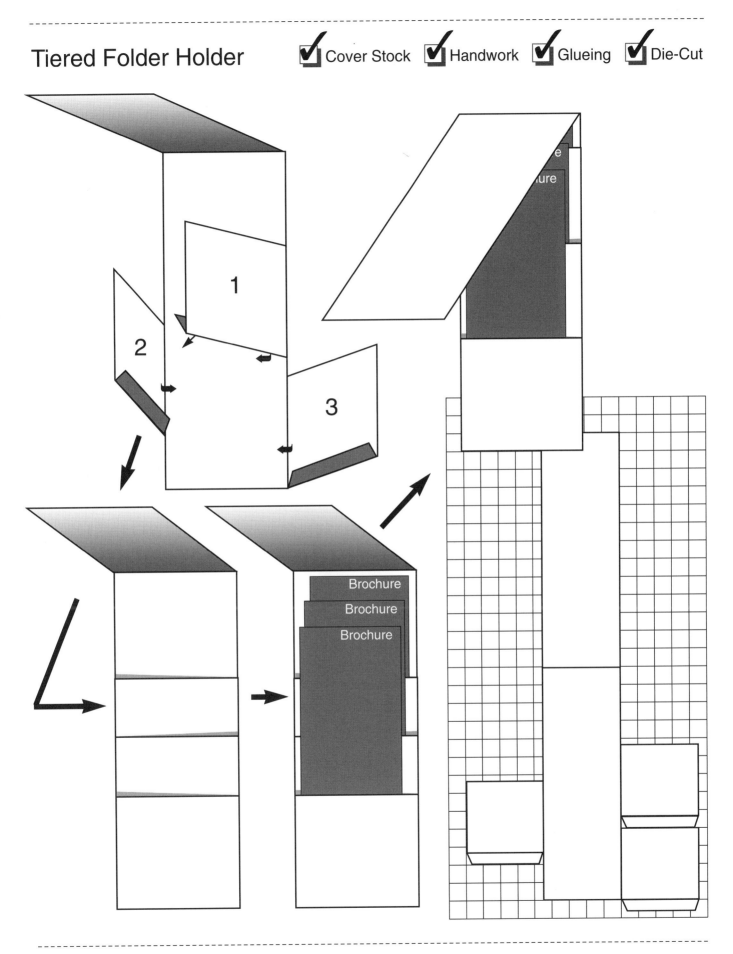

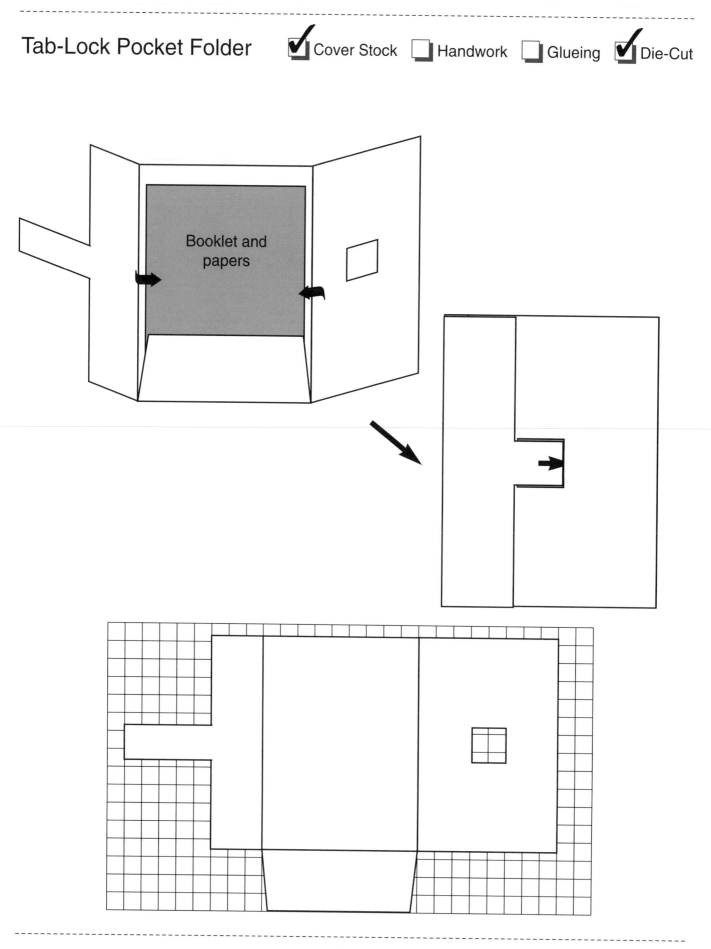

Booklet and papers

# Accordion Folder Folder

☑ Cover Stock ☑ Handwork ☑ Glueing ☑ Die-Cut

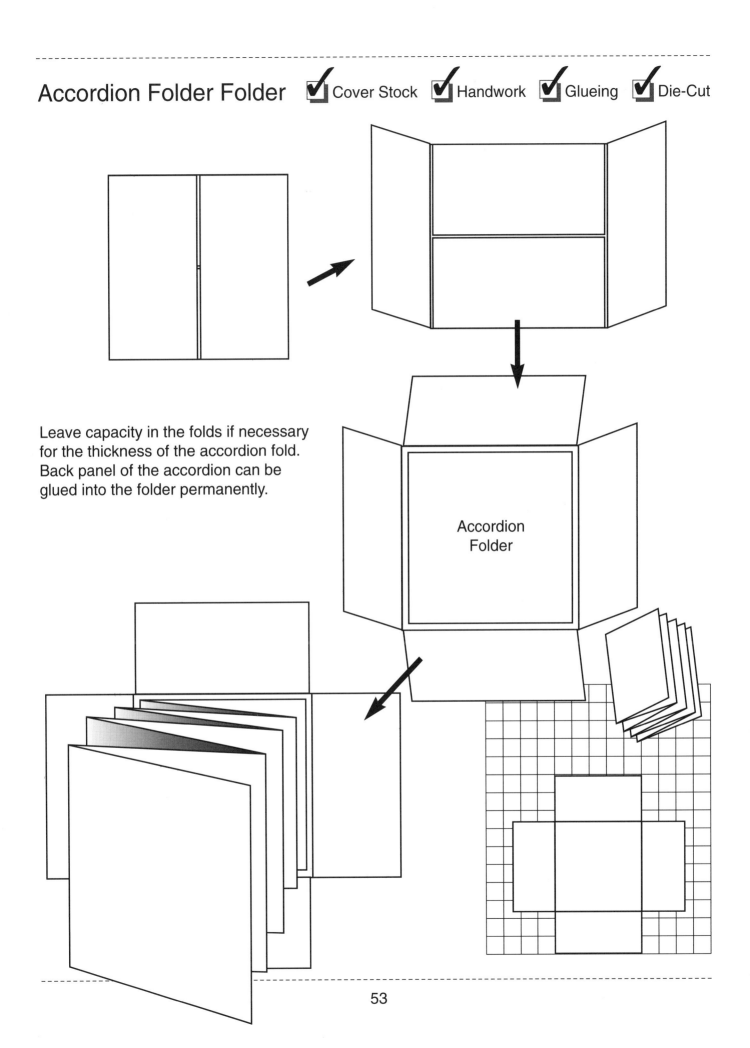

Leave capacity in the folds if necessary for the thickness of the accordion fold. Back panel of the accordion can be glued into the folder permanently.

Accordion Folder

# Portfolio Folder

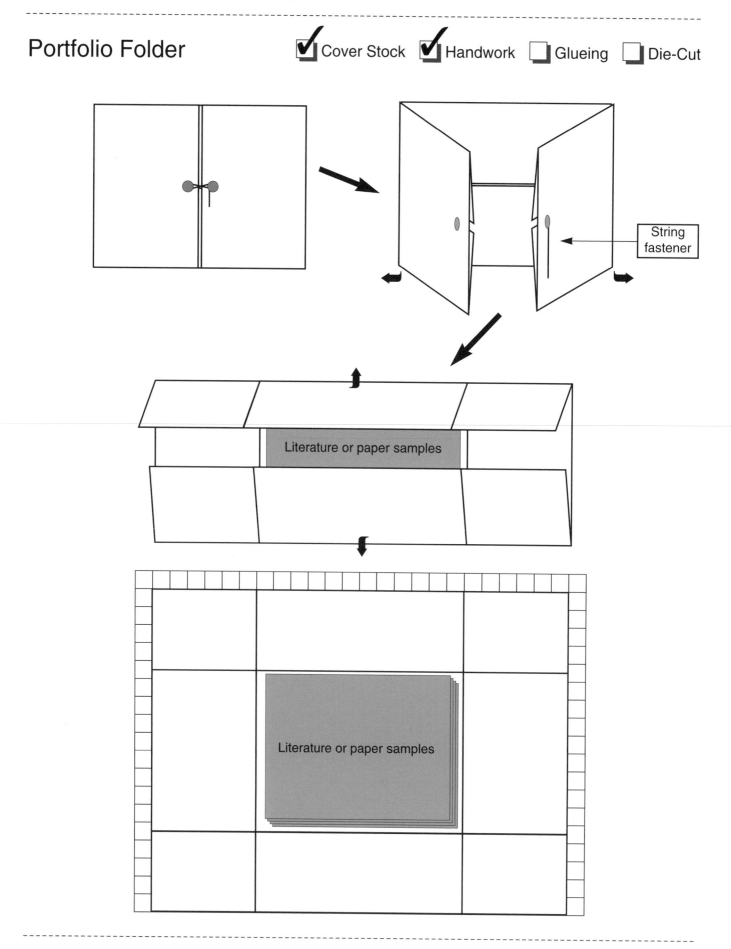

String fastener

Literature or paper samples

Literature or paper samples

# Tab Locking Portfolio

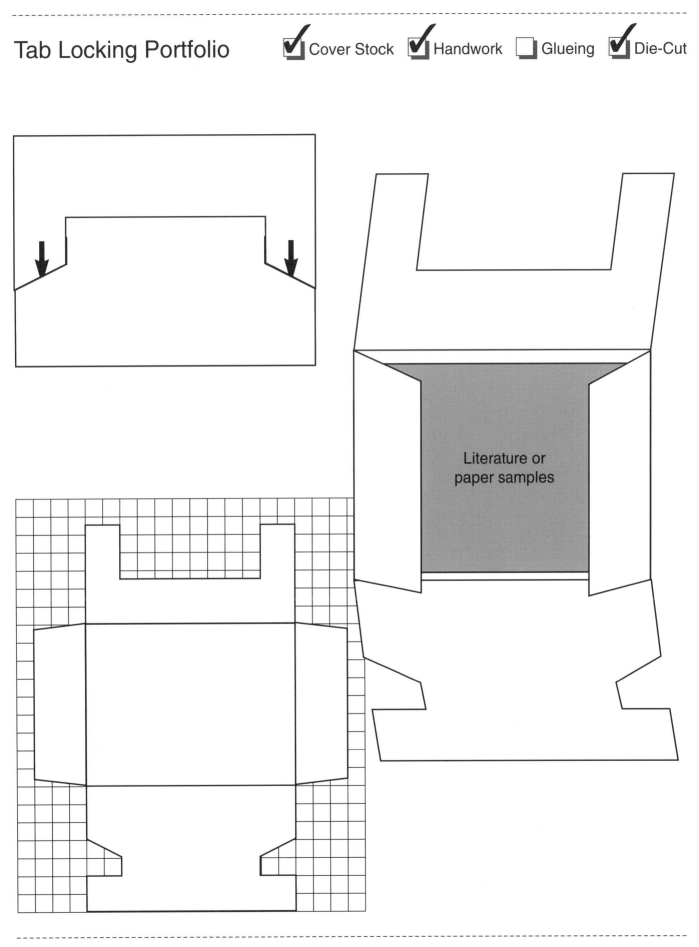

Literature or paper samples

# GREETING CARDS

## Locking Folder

Cover Stock ✓ Handwork ✓ Glueing ☐ Die-Cut ✓

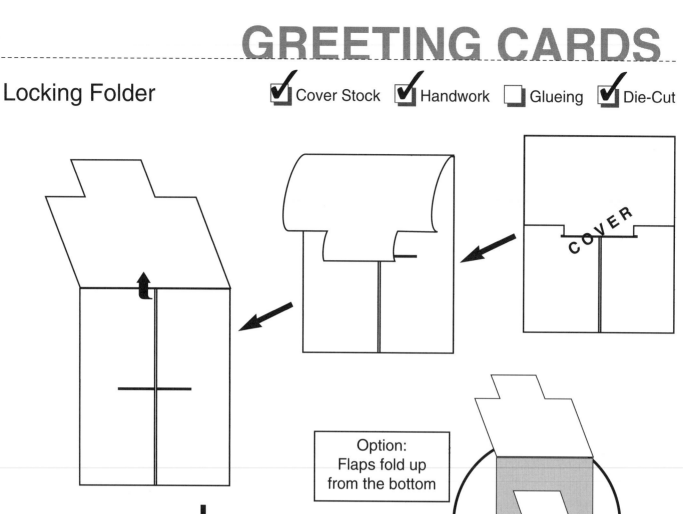

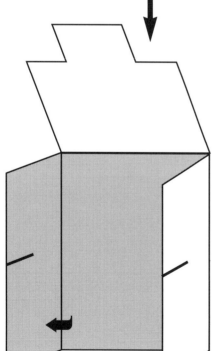

Option:
Flaps fold up
from the bottom

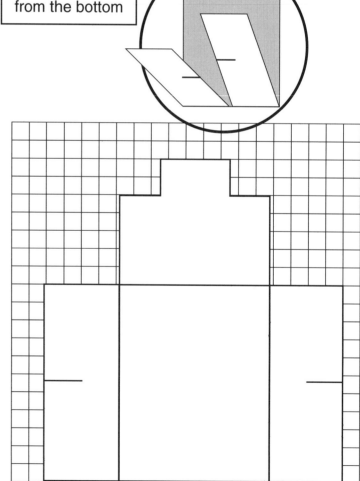

# Barndoor Folder/Greeting Card

☑ Cover Stock ☐ Handwork ☐ Glueing ☑ Die-Cut

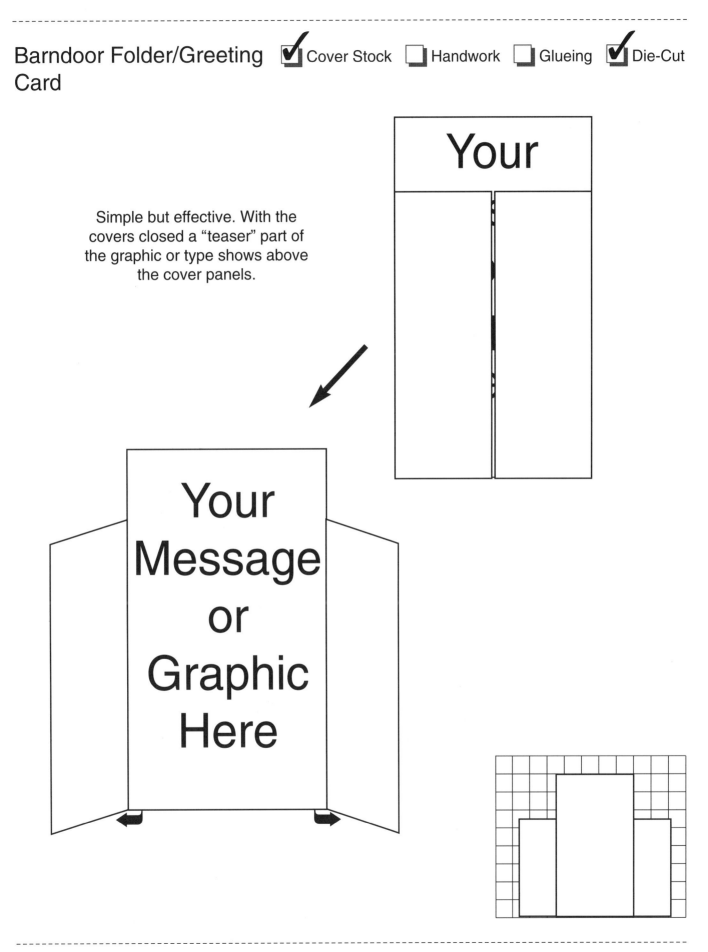

Simple but effective. With the covers closed a "teaser" part of the graphic or type shows above the cover panels.

Your

Your Message or Graphic Here

# Greeting Card

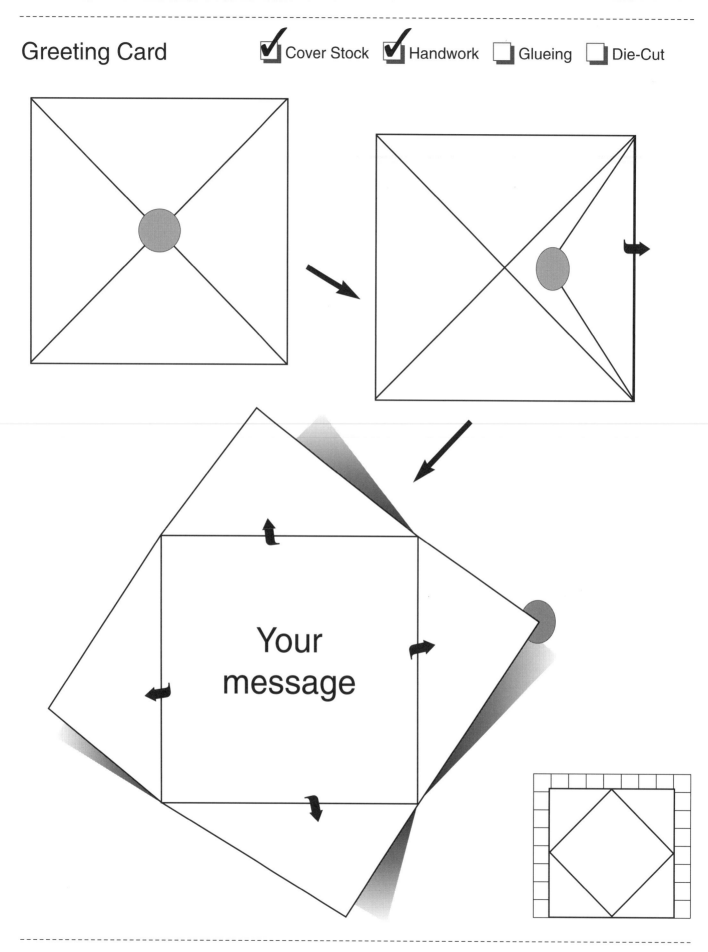

Your message

## CD Mailer

☑ Cover Stock  ☑ Handwork  ☐ Glueing  ☑ Die-Cut

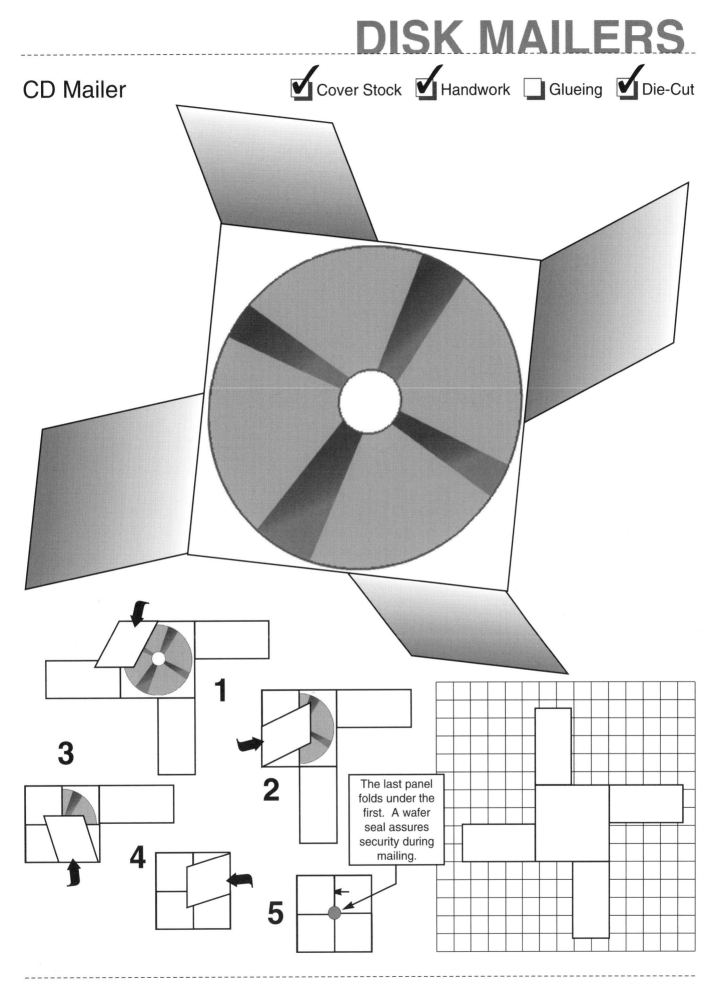

**1**

**2**

**3**

**4**

**5**

The last panel folds under the first. A wafer seal assures security during mailing.

# CD Mailer

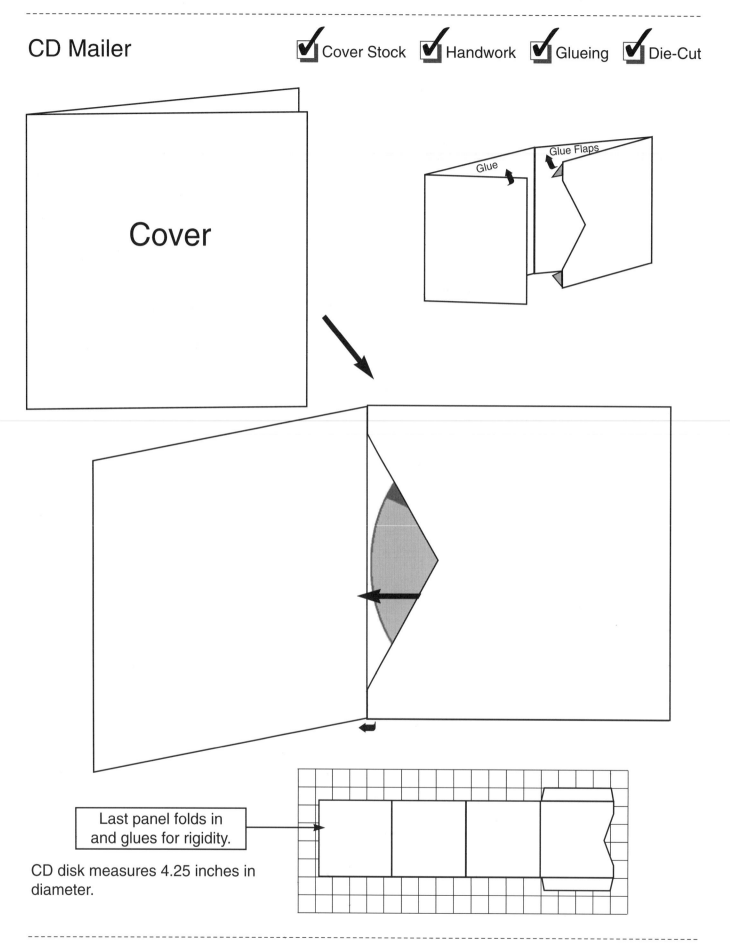

Cover

Glue

Glue Flaps

Last panel folds in and glues for rigidity.

CD disk measures 4.25 inches in diameter.

# Floppy Disk Mailer

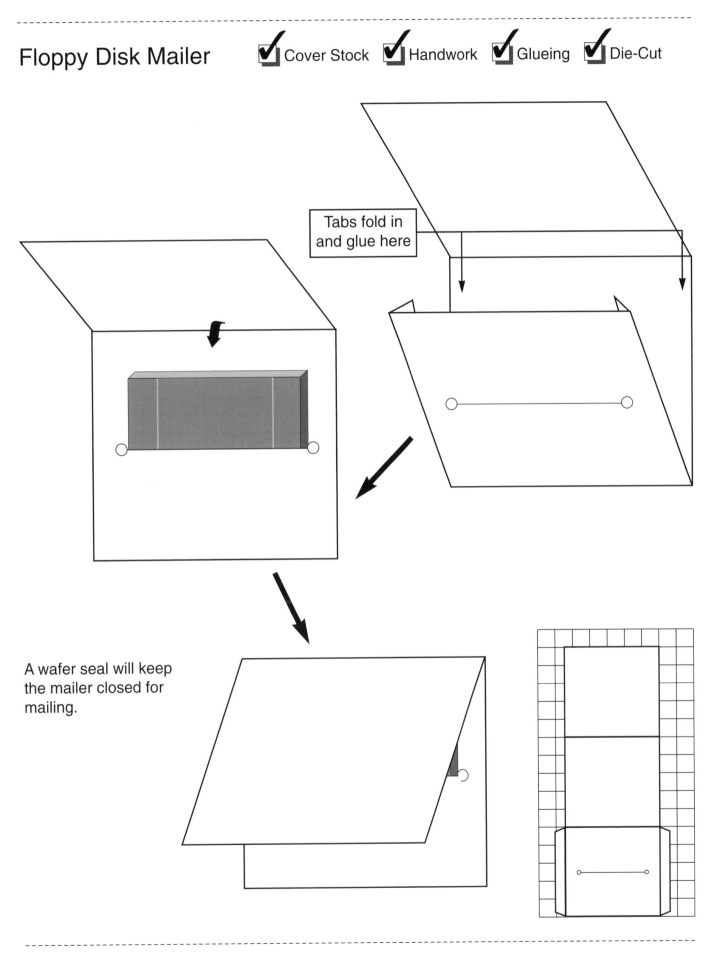

Tabs fold in and glue here

A wafer seal will keep the mailer closed for mailing.

# CD Mailer

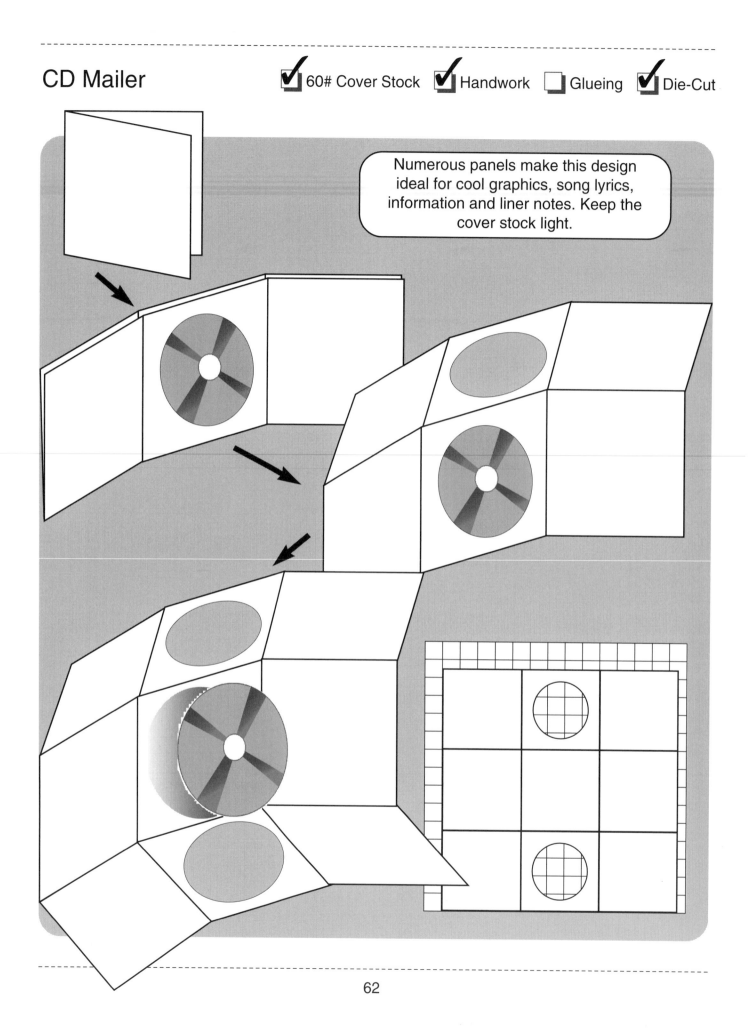

Numerous panels make this design ideal for cool graphics, song lyrics, information and liner notes. Keep the cover stock light.

# Corner slot disk holder

Scan Disk

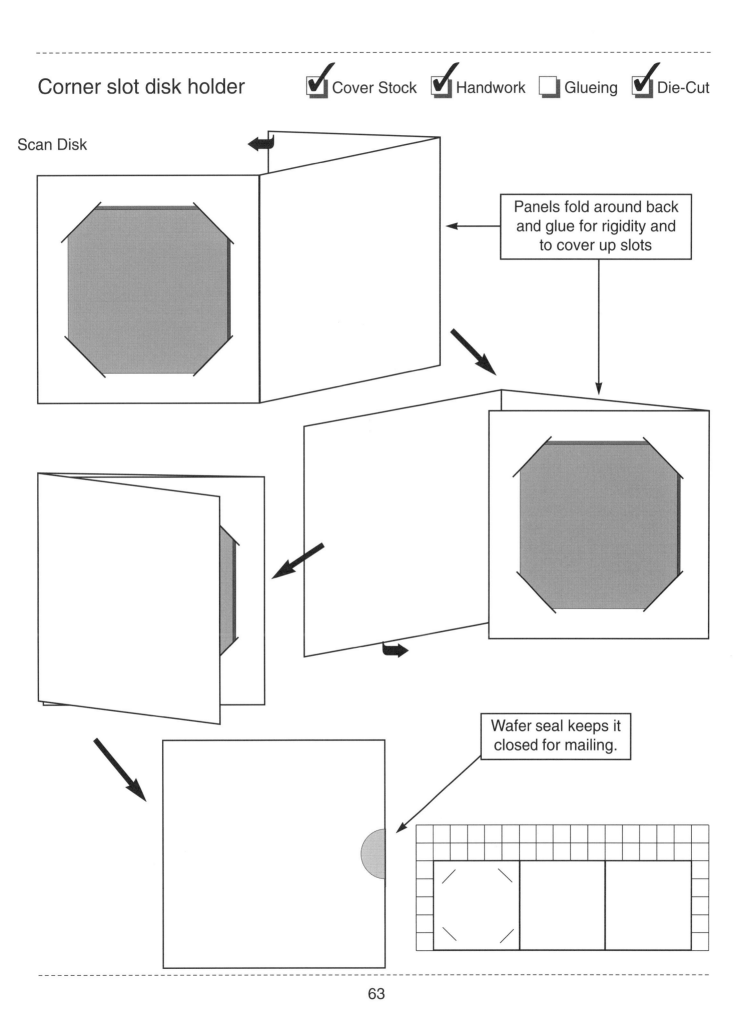

Panels fold around back and glue for rigidity and to cover up slots

Wafer seal keeps it closed for mailing.

# Two CD Jacket

☑ Text Cover Stock ☑ Handwork ☐ Glueing ☑ Die-Cut

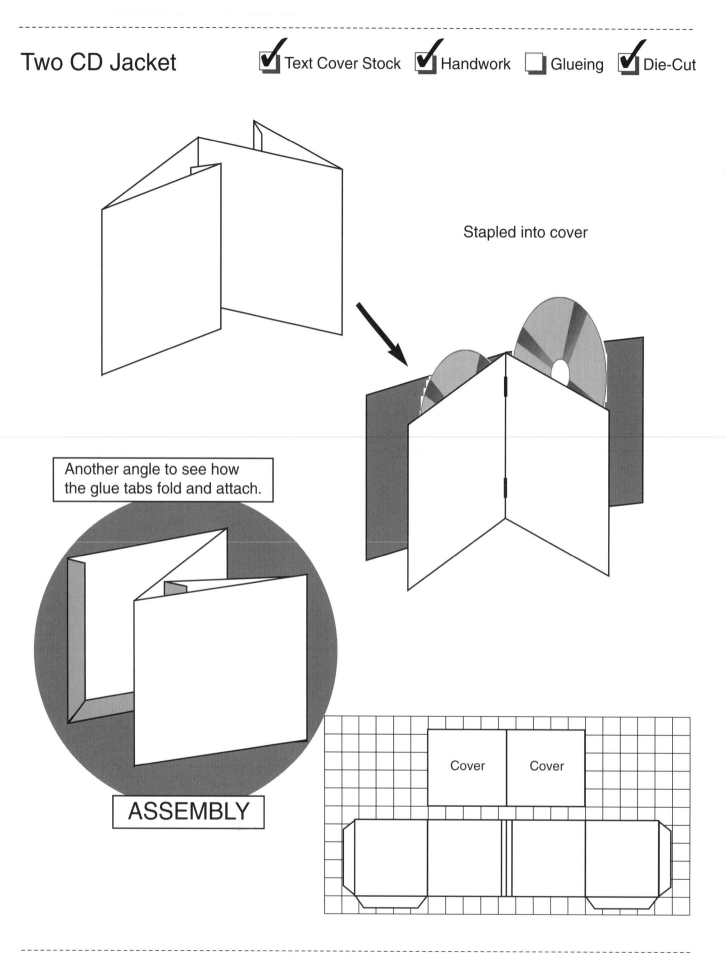

Stapled into cover

Another angle to see how
the glue tabs fold and attach.

ASSEMBLY

Cover | Cover

# Floppy Disk Mailer

☑ Text Cover Stock  ☑ Handwork  ☑ Glueing  ☑ Die-Cut

The measurements for this piece are critical. Provide capacity as the stock is thick. The die cut holes on panels A and C are slightly larger than the size of a standard floppy disk. The die-cut hole of panel B measures the exact dimensions of a floppy disk and holds the disk snuggly in place. Panel C folds in first and glues on panel B. Panel A then folds in and glues to panel C. Next panels A-B-C fold in and glue to panel D. Finally, panel E folds in and covers the floppy disk.

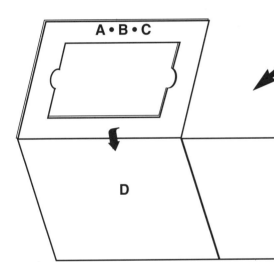

The combination of three die-cutpanels stacked one on another is designed to accomodate the depth of the floppy disk.

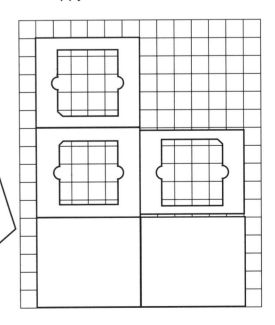

Put disk in place.
Then cover mailer.

# CD Mailer

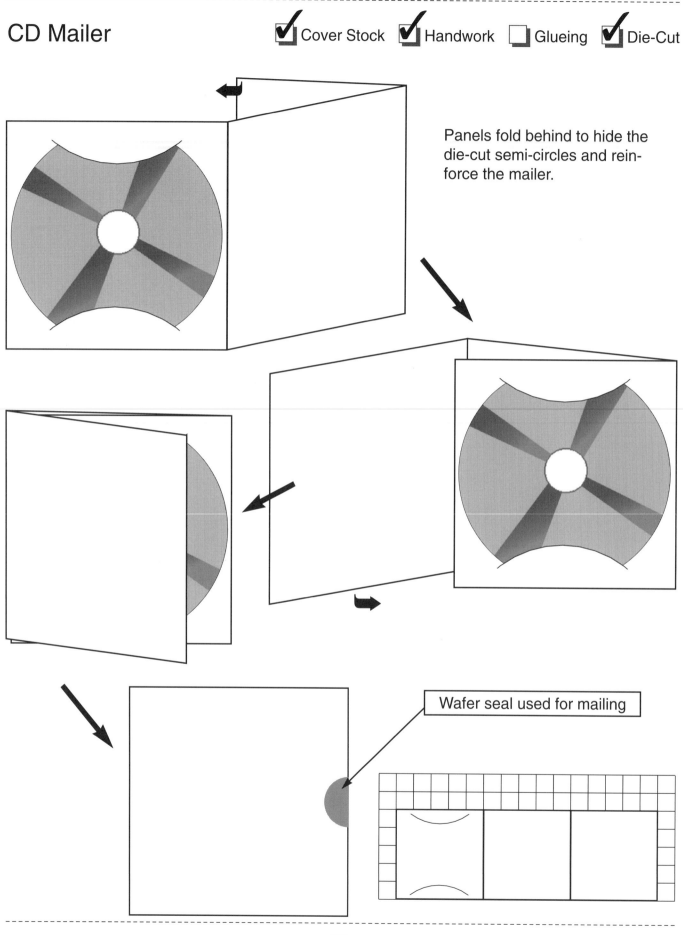

Panels fold behind to hide the die-cut semi-circles and reinforce the mailer.

Wafer seal used for mailing

## Take-One Poster

☑ Cover Stock  ☑ Handwork  ☑ Glueing  ☑ Die-Cut

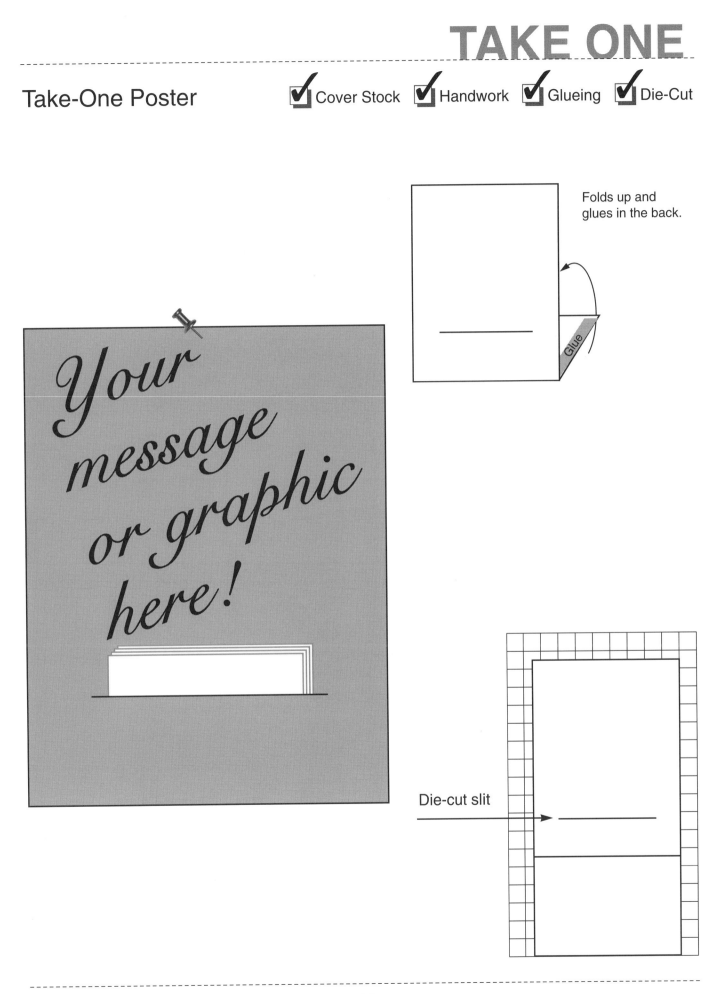

Folds up and glues in the back.

Glue

*Your message or graphic here!*

Die-cut slit

# Take-one BRC Holder

☑ Cover Stock  ☑ Handwork  ☑ Glueing  ☑ Die-Cut

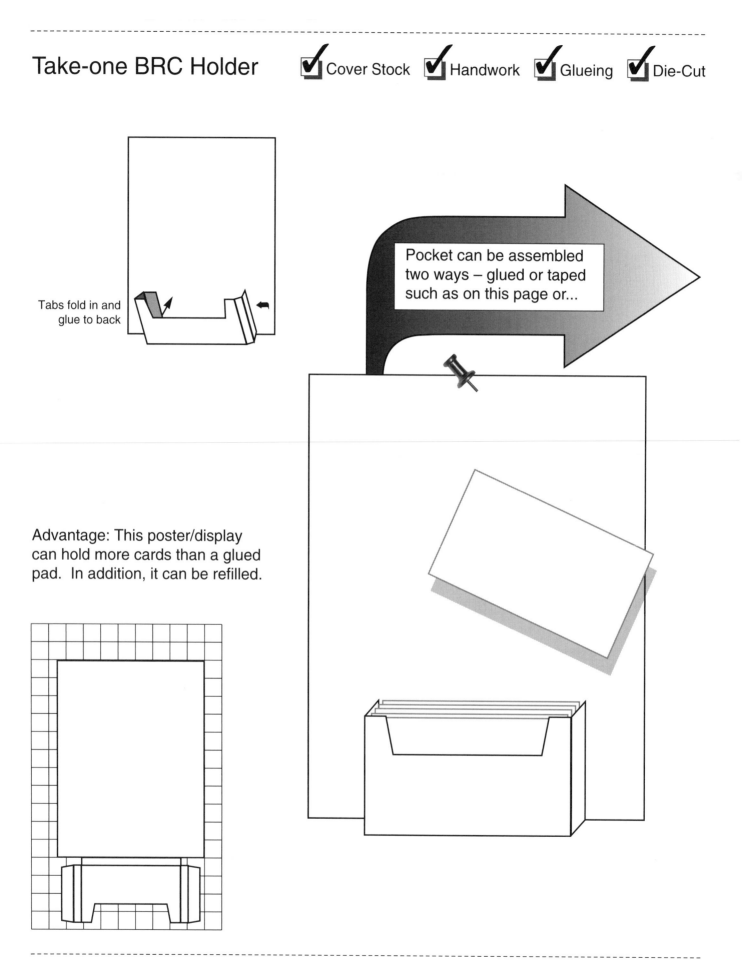

Tabs fold in and glue to back

Pocket can be assembled two ways – glued or taped such as on this page or...

Advantage: This poster/display can hold more cards than a glued pad. In addition, it can be refilled.

☑ Text Cover Stock  ☑ Handwork  ☐ Glueing  ☑ Die-Cut

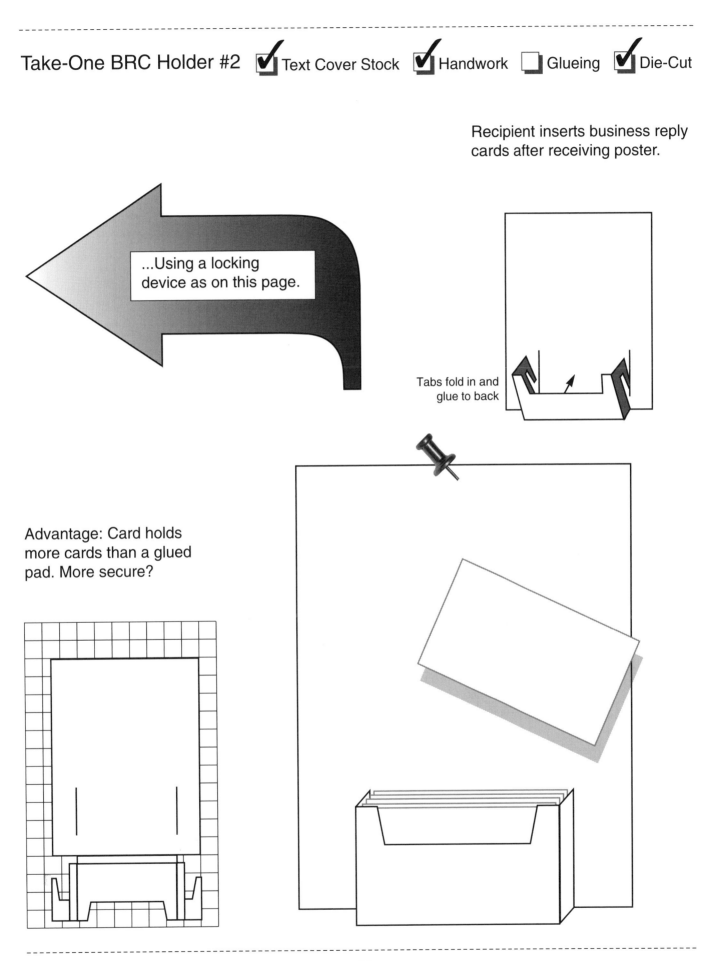

...Using a locking device as on this page.

Recipient inserts business reply cards after receiving poster.

Tabs fold in and glue to back

Advantage: Card holds more cards than a glued pad. More secure?

The benefit of the design is its simplicity, although its capacity is limited depending on the number of folders and the thickness of those pieces.

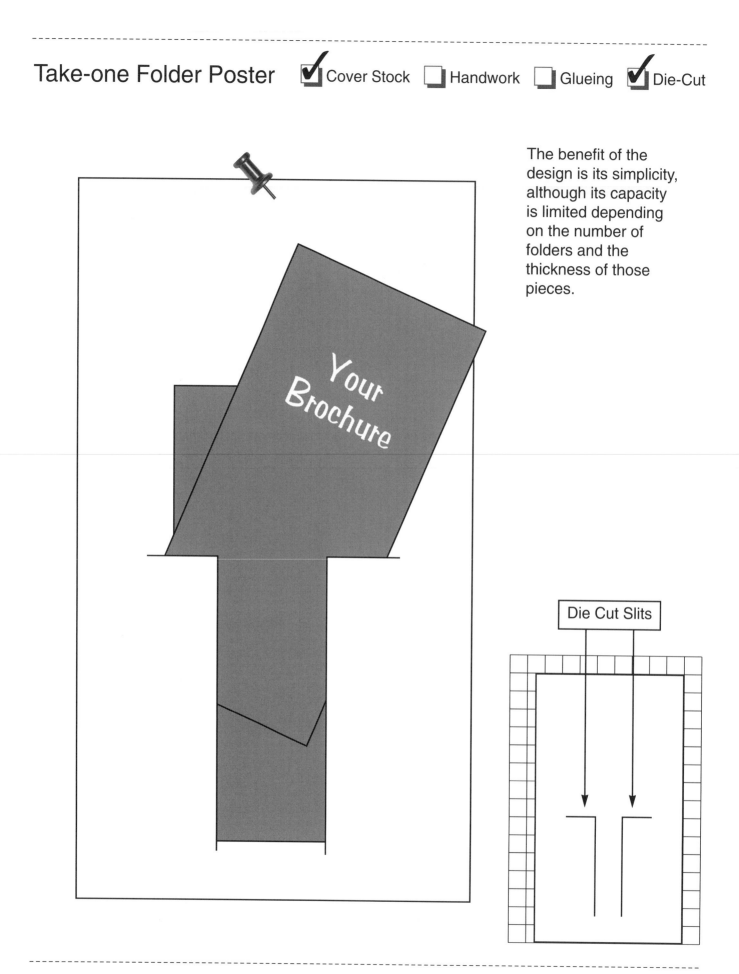

Your Brochure

Die Cut Slits

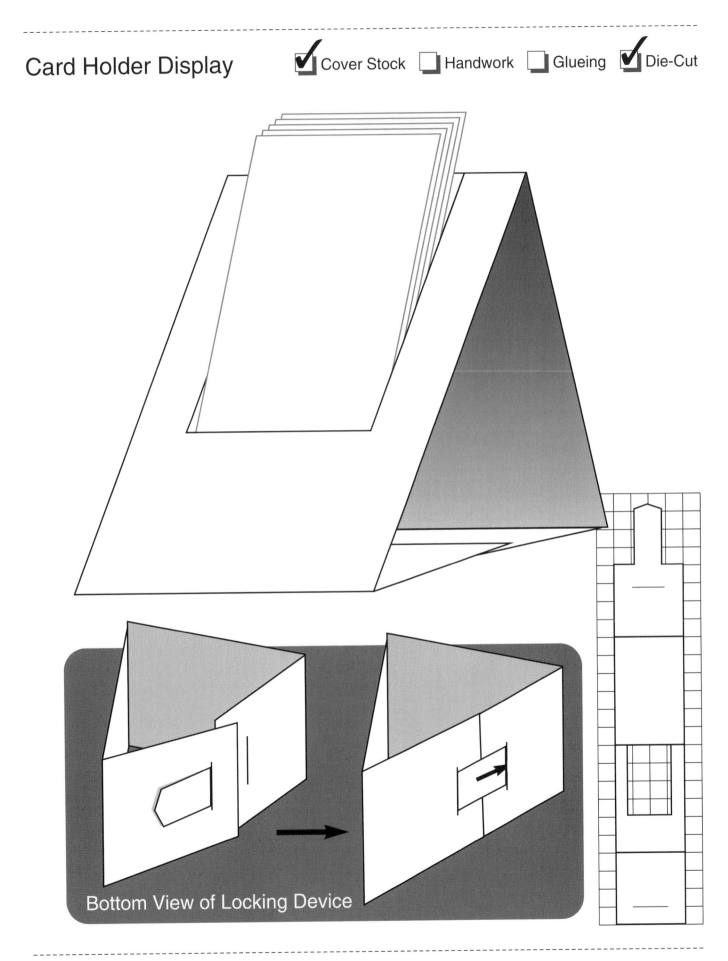

Bottom View of Locking Device

# Take-One Folder Holder

☑ Cover Stock  ☑ Handwork  ☐ Glueing  ☑ Die-Cut

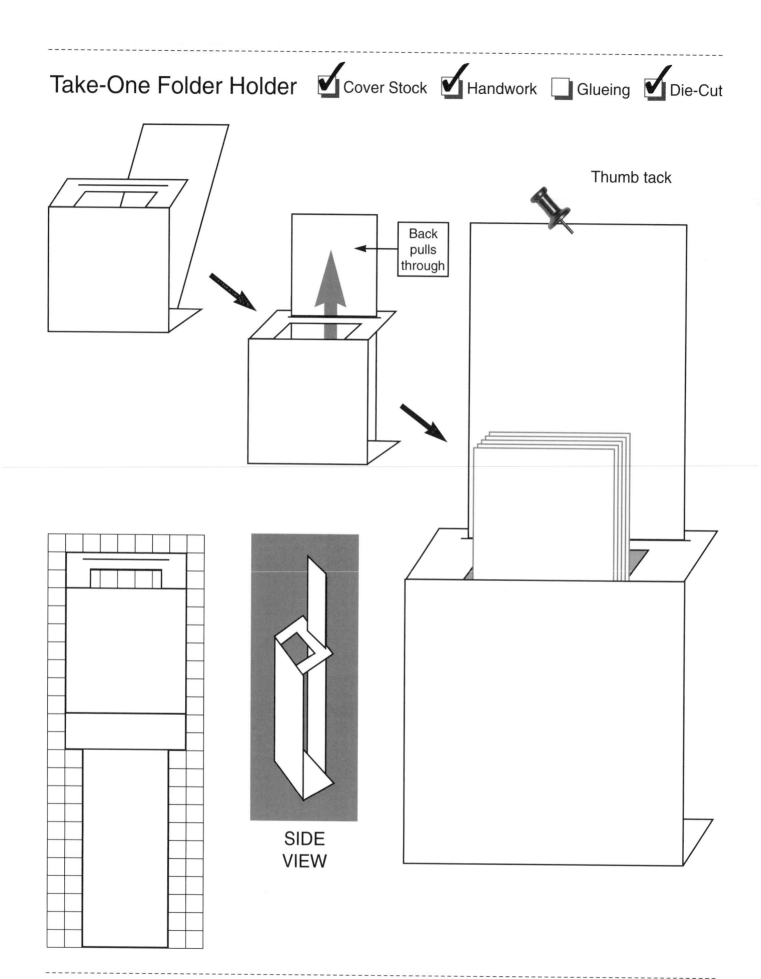

Thumb tack

Back pulls through

SIDE
VIEW

# Self-mailing take-one poster

☑ Cover Stock ☑ Handwork ☑ Glueing ☑ Die-Cut

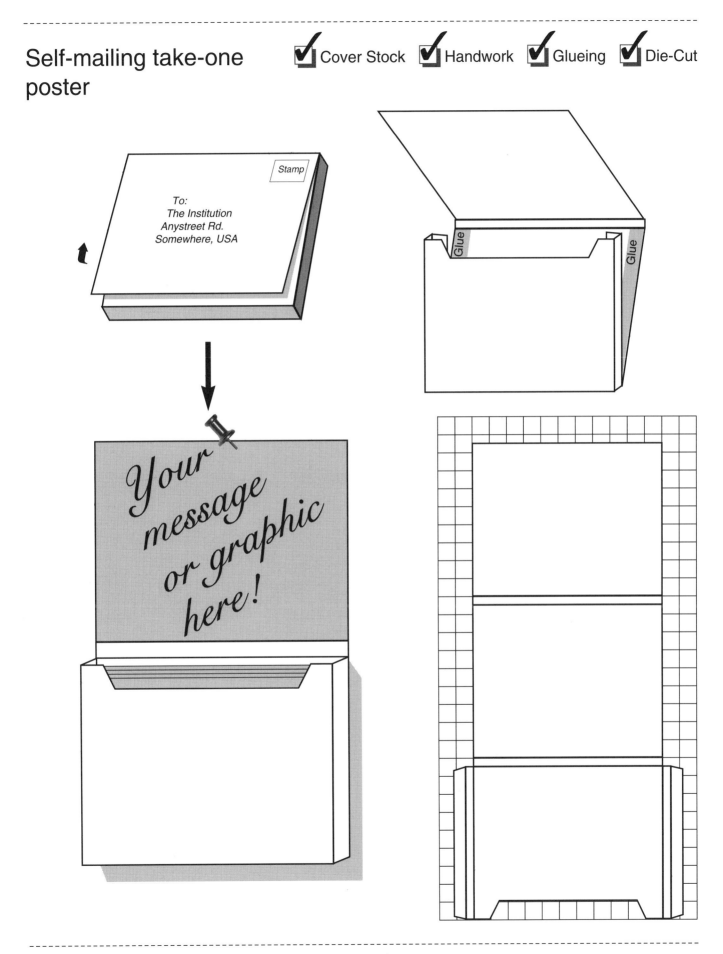

# Self-Assembling Easel

☑ 10pt Cover Stock  ☑ Handwork  ☑ Glueing  ☑ Die-Cut

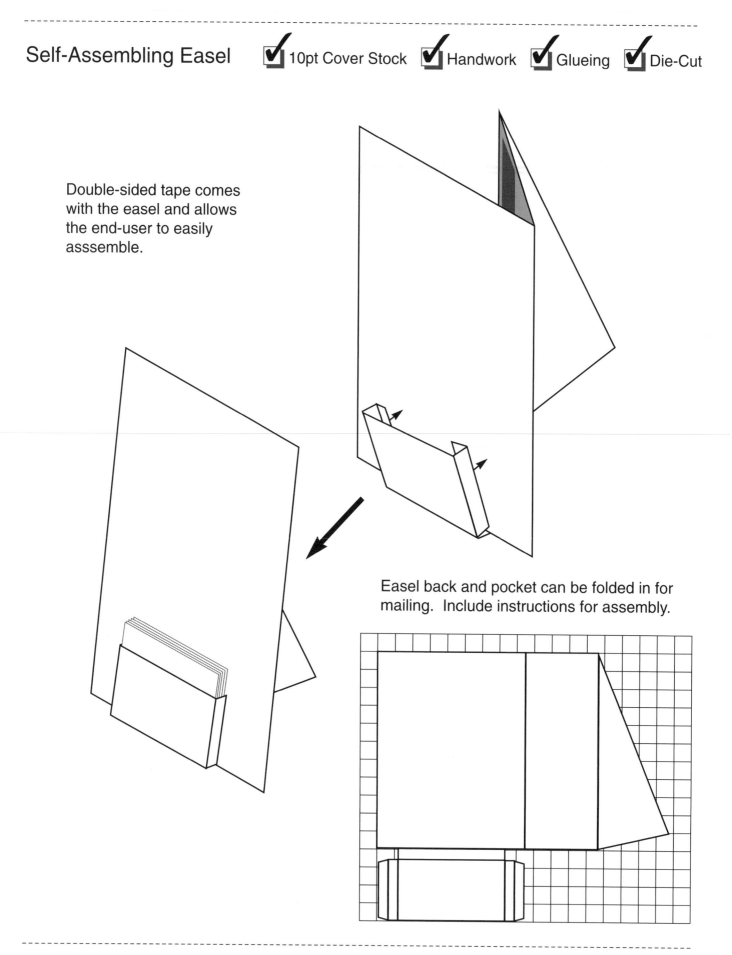

Double-sided tape comes with the easel and allows the end-user to easily asssemble.

Easel back and pocket can be folded in for mailing.  Include instructions for assembly.

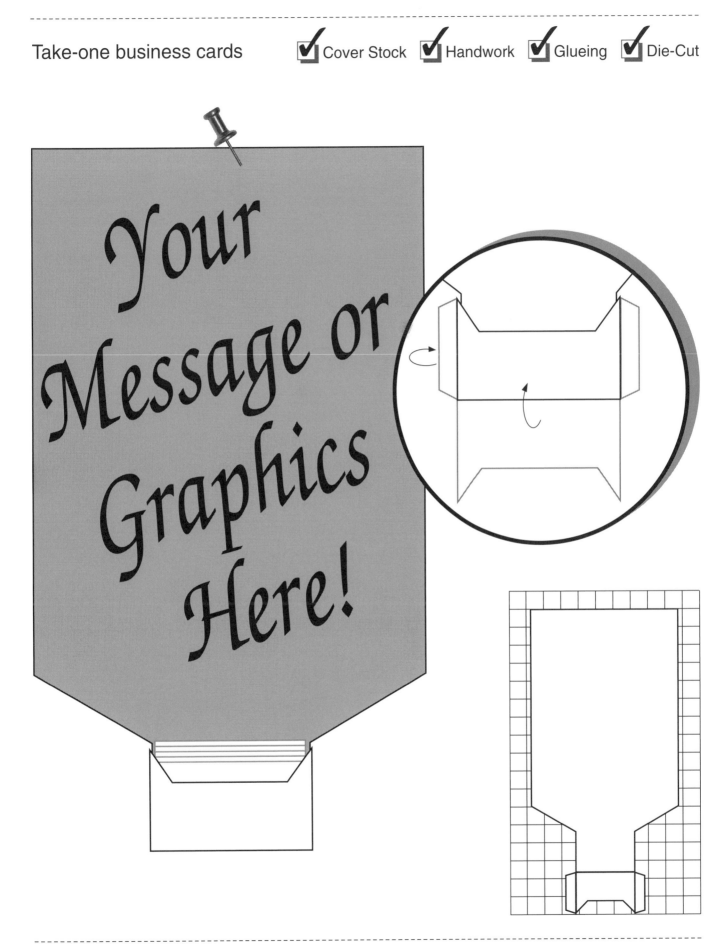

# Take-one Easle Display

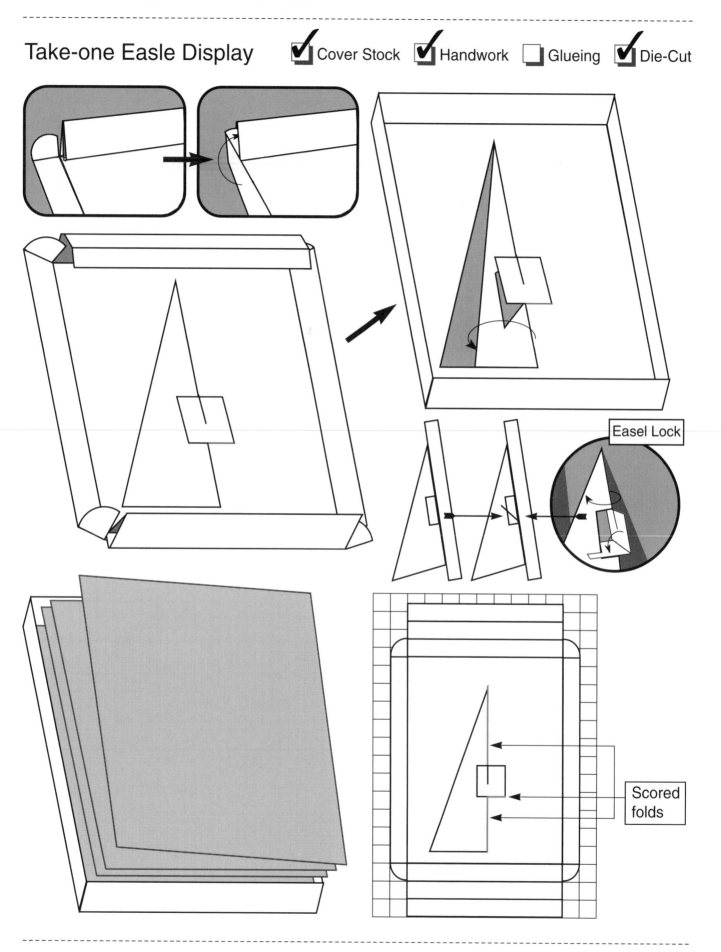

Easel Lock

Scored folds

# Booklet Dispenser

☑ Cover Stock  ☑ Handwork  ☑ Glueing  ☑ Die-Cut

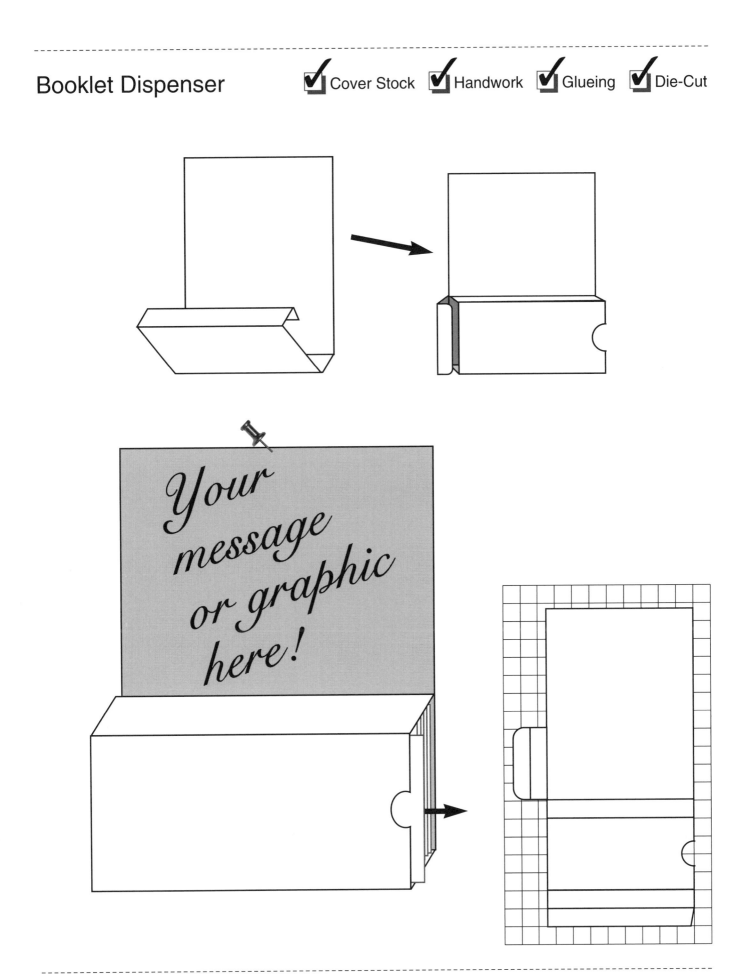

*Your message or graphic here!*

☑ Cover Stock  ☑ Handwork  ☑ Glueing  ☑ Die-Cut

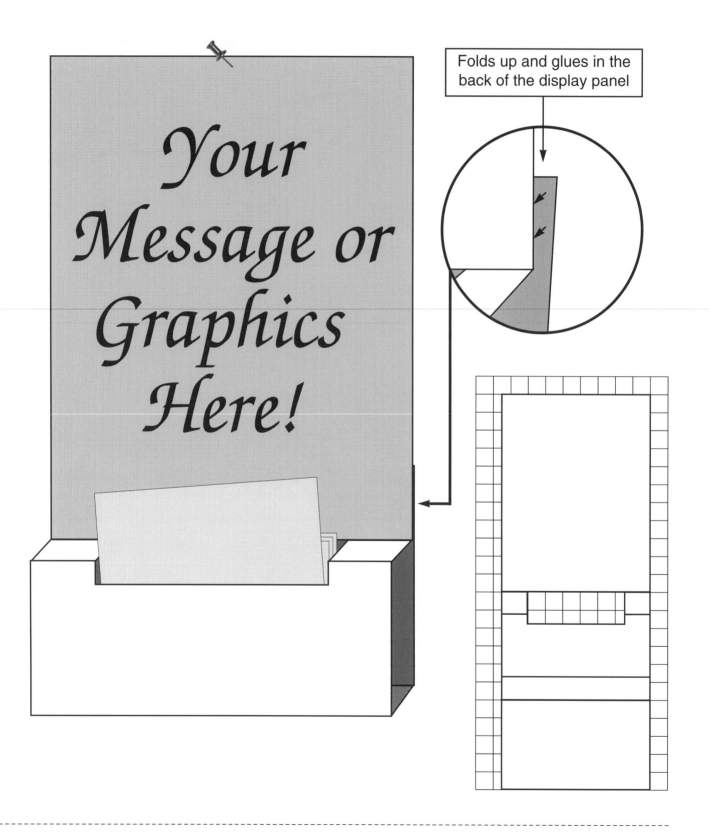

Folds up and glues in the back of the display panel

*Your Message or Graphics Here!*

☑ Cover Stock ☑ Handwork ☐ Glueing ☑ Die-Cut

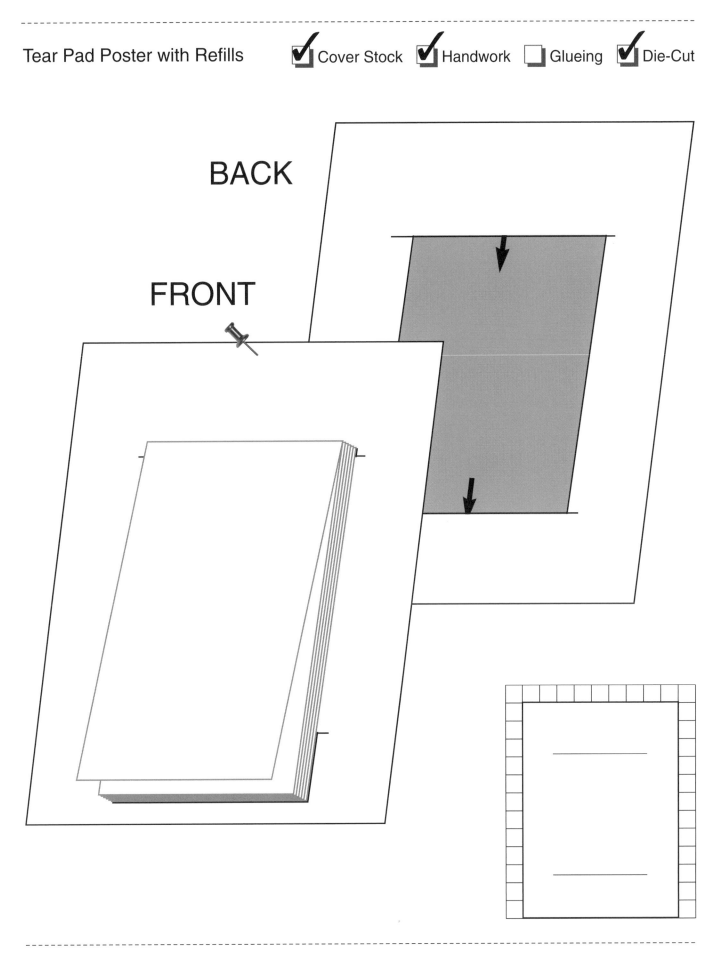

BACK

FRONT

## Accordion Pop-up

☑ Cover Stock ☑ Handwork ☐ Glueing ☑ Die-Cut

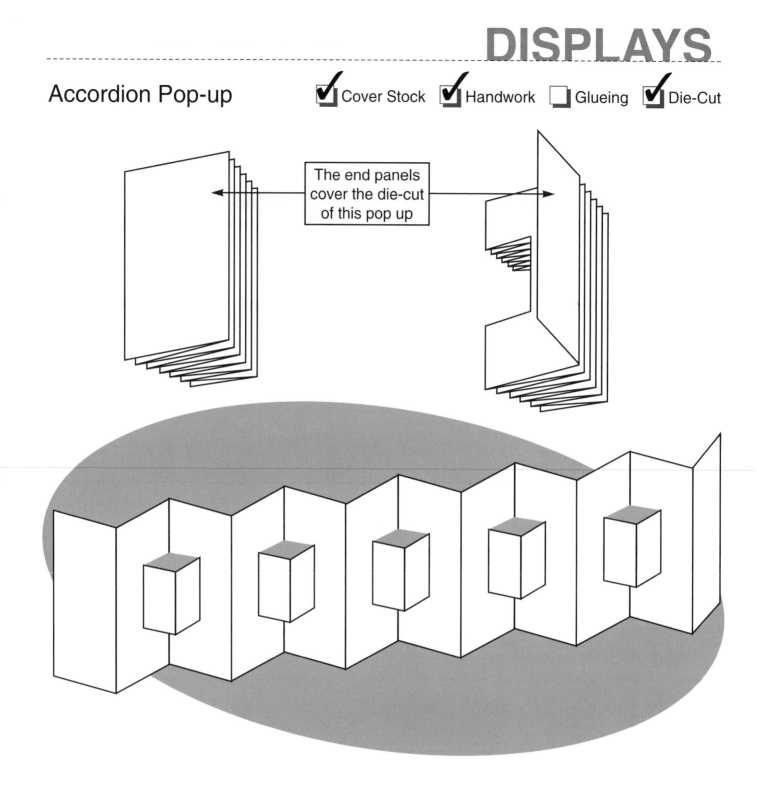

The end panels cover the die-cut of this pop up

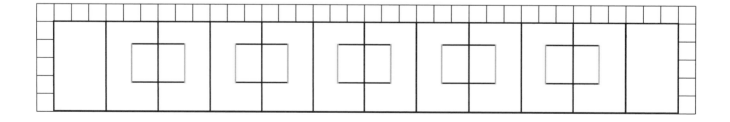

# Standing Pop-up

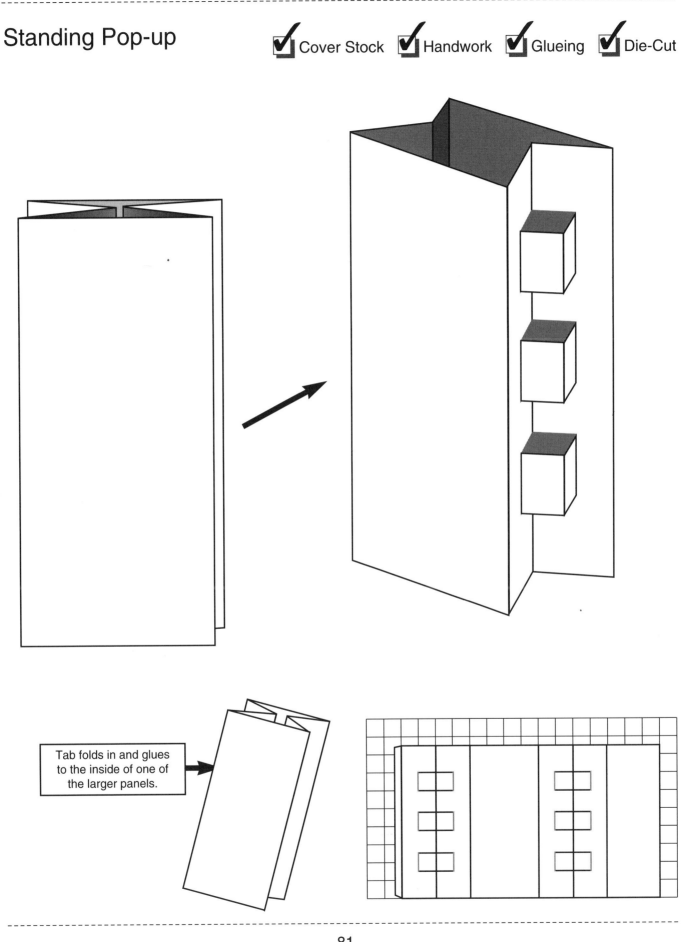

Tab folds in and glues to the inside of one of the larger panels.

# Diarama display

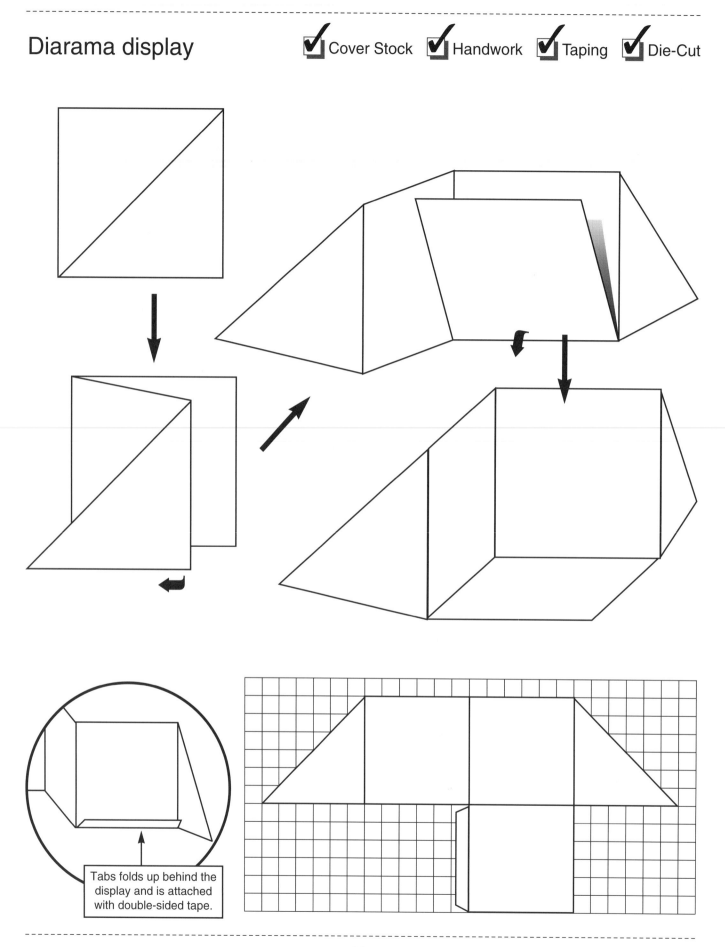

Tabs folds up behind the display and is attached with double-sided tape.

# Table Tent

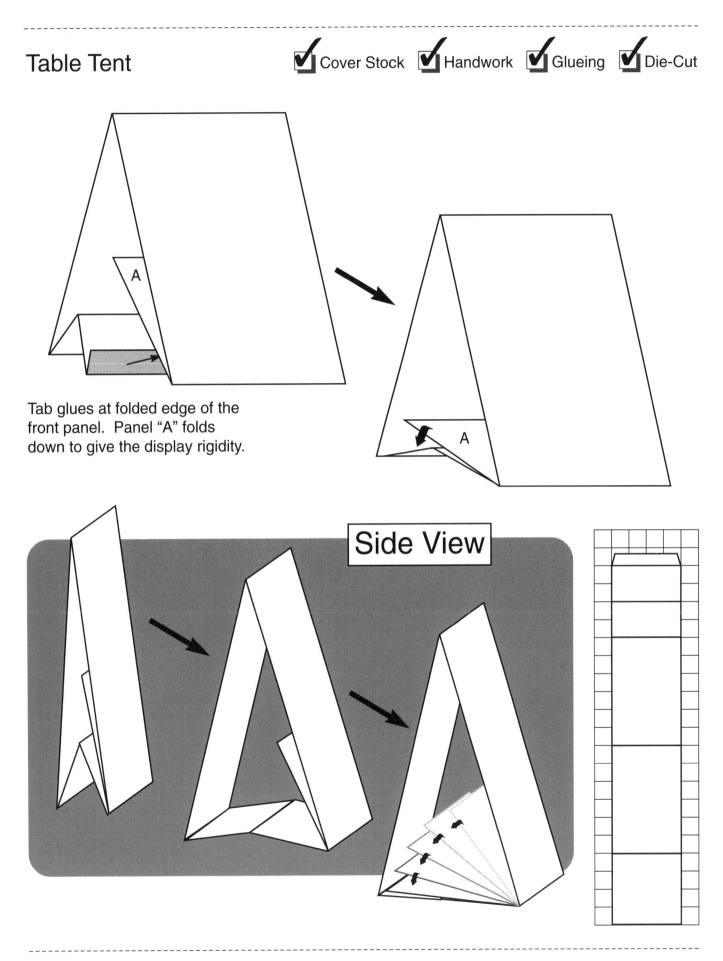

Tab glues at folded edge of the front panel. Panel "A" folds down to give the display rigidity.

Side View

# Pop-Up Display

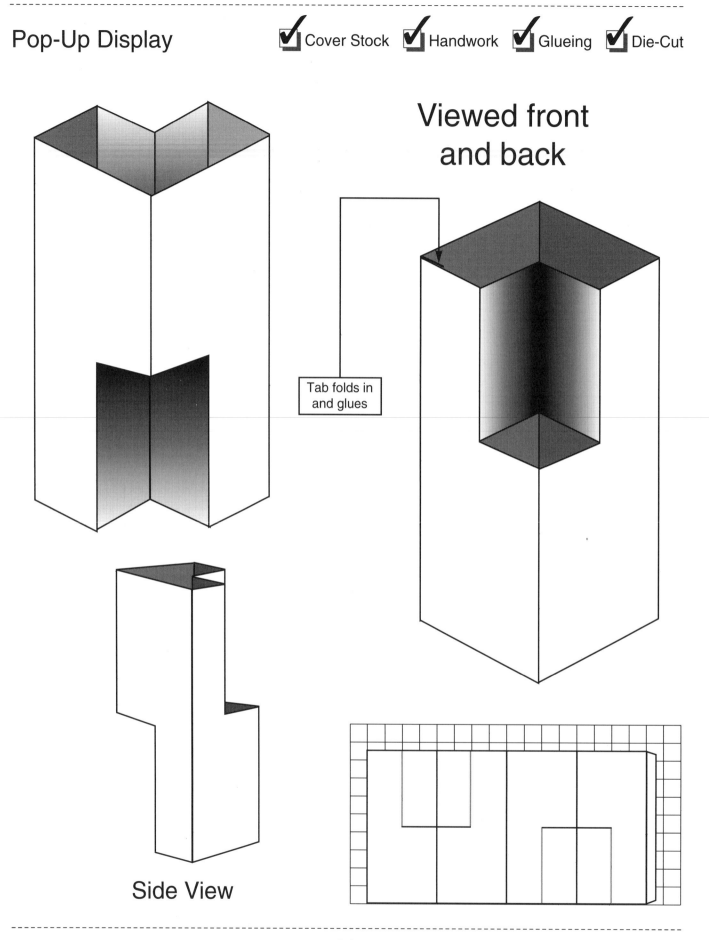

Viewed front and back

Tab folds in and glues

Side View

Die-Cut Display · Cover Stock · Handwork · Glueing · Die-Cut

Glue or double-stick tape

WRITE

YOUR

MESSAGE

HERE

!!!!!!!!!!!!

Tab folds around and either glues or tapes.

YOUR

# Fold-Out Table Tent

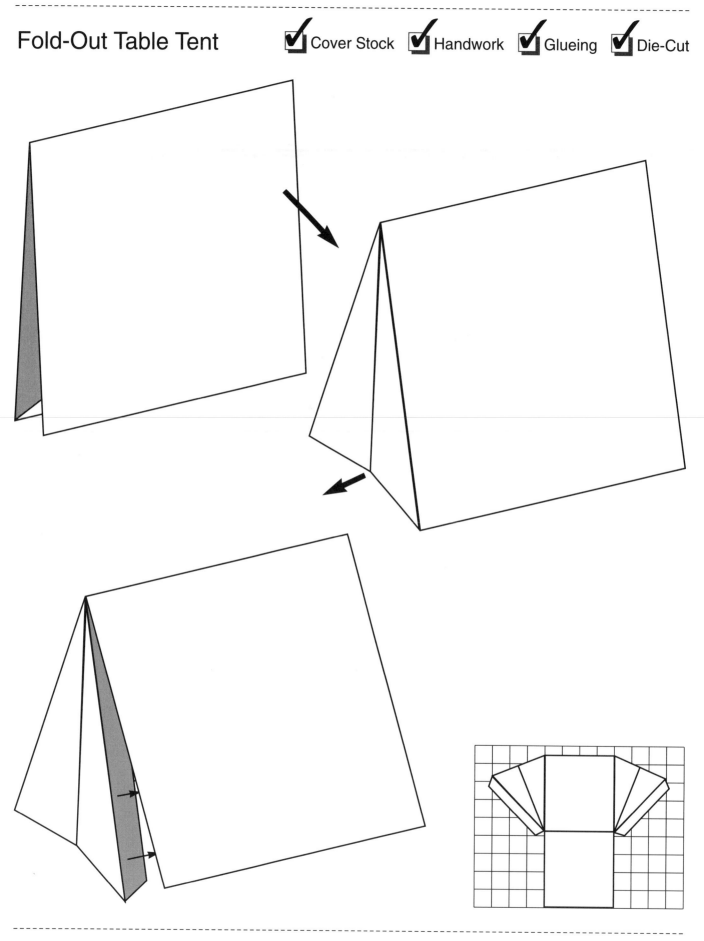

# Matchbook Table Top Display

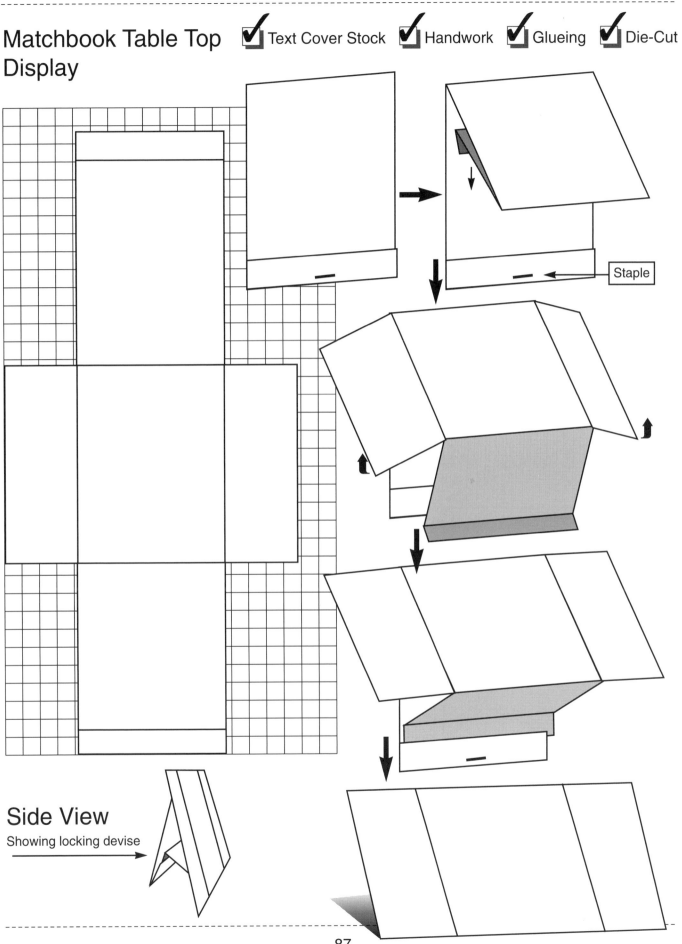

Staple

## Side View
Showing locking devise

Cover Stock  Handwork  Glueing  Die-Cut

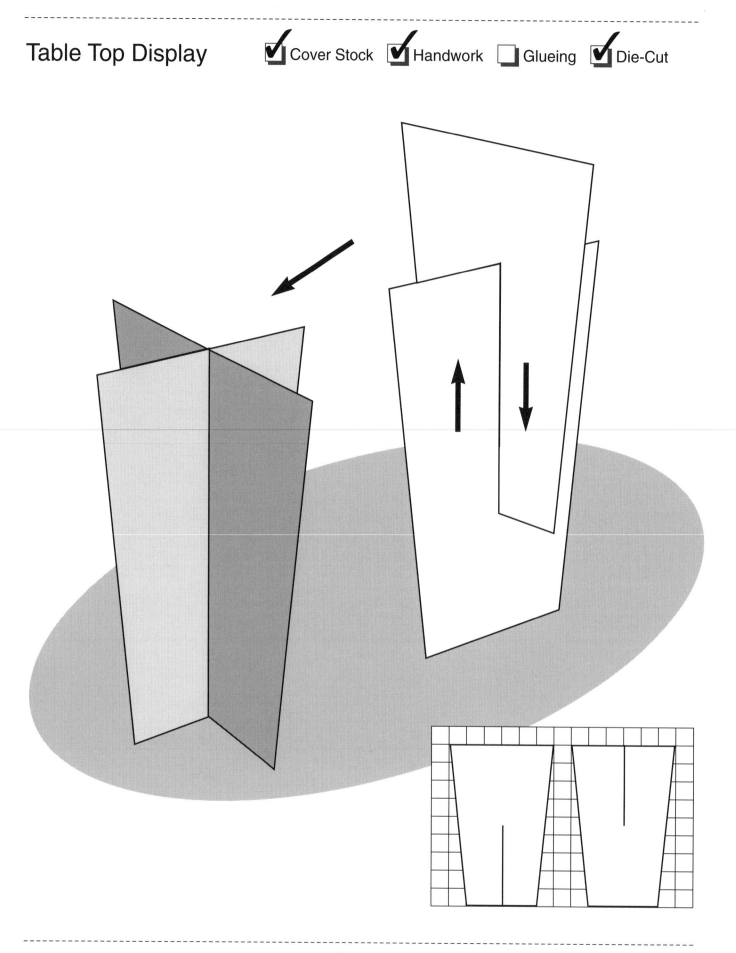

# Cone Table Top Car Display

☑Cover Stock  ☑Handwork  ☑Taping  ☑Die-Cut

Vary the diameter of the base and size of the display card.  The angle of the die-cut determines the angle of the slant of the display card.

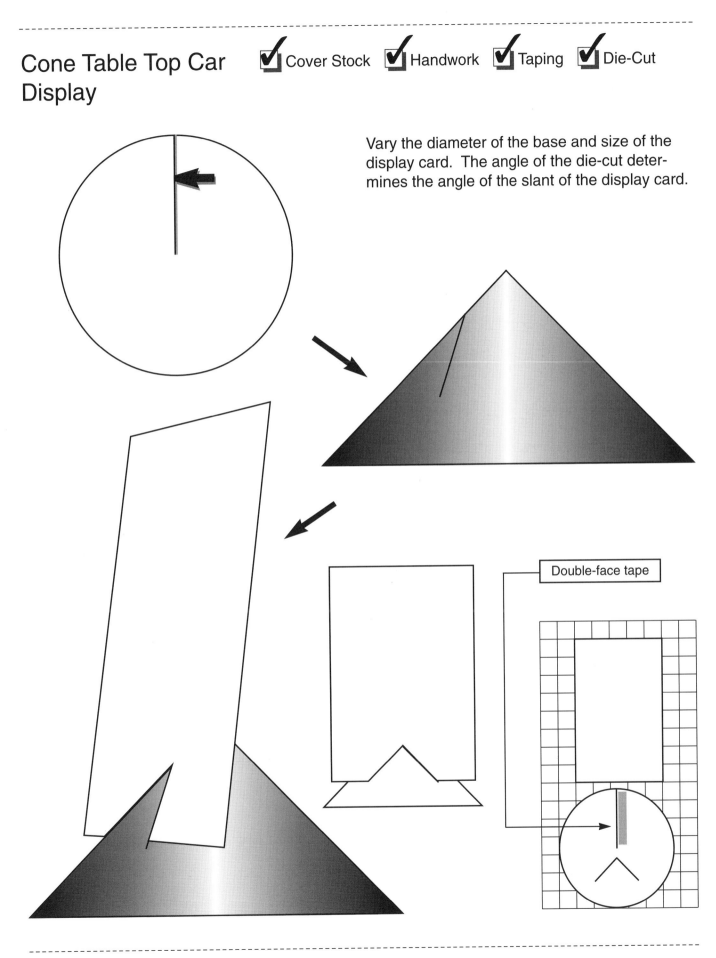

Double-face tape

Cover Stock ☑ Handwork ☑ Glueing ☐ Die-Cut ☑

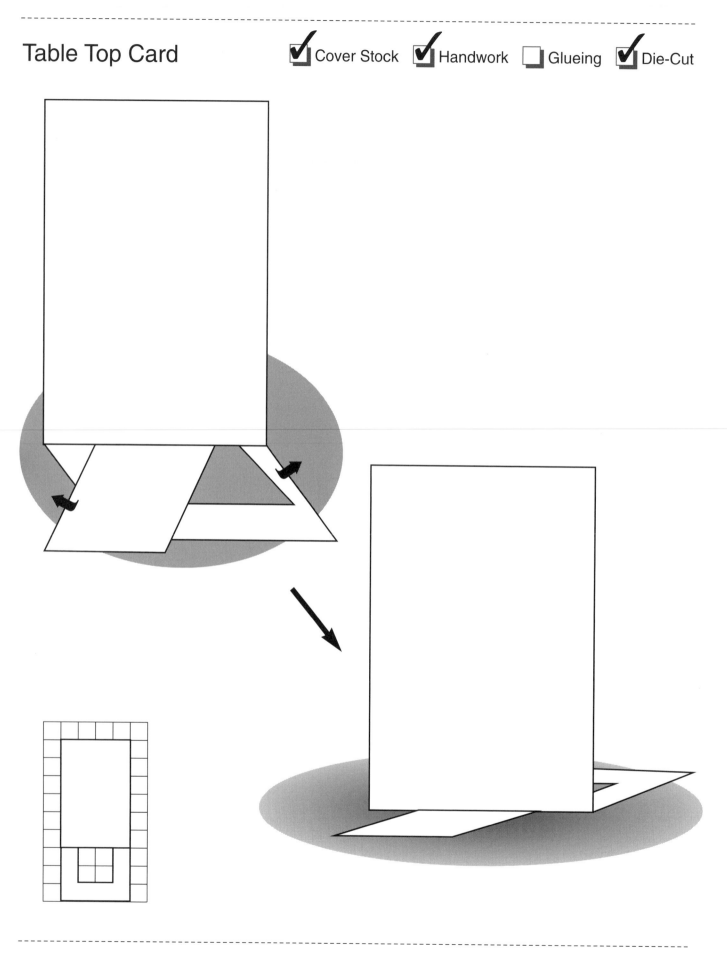

# Table Top Card Display    ☑ Cover Stock  ☑ Handwork  ☐ Glueing  ☑ Die-Cut

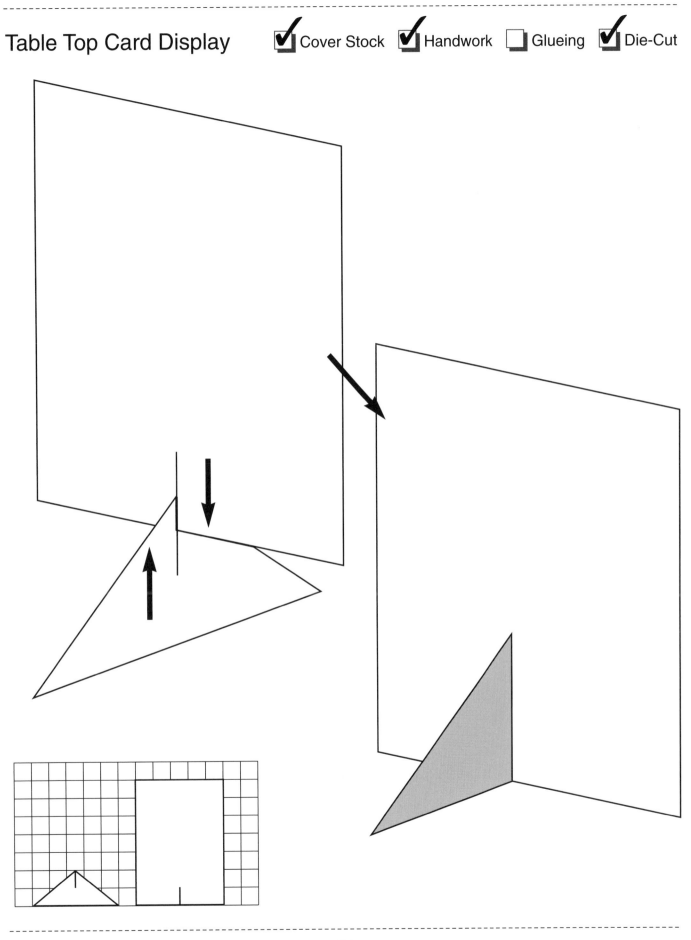

# Self-mailing Easel & Booklet Display

☑ Text & Cover Stock  ☑ Handwork  ☐ Glueing  ☑ Die-Cut

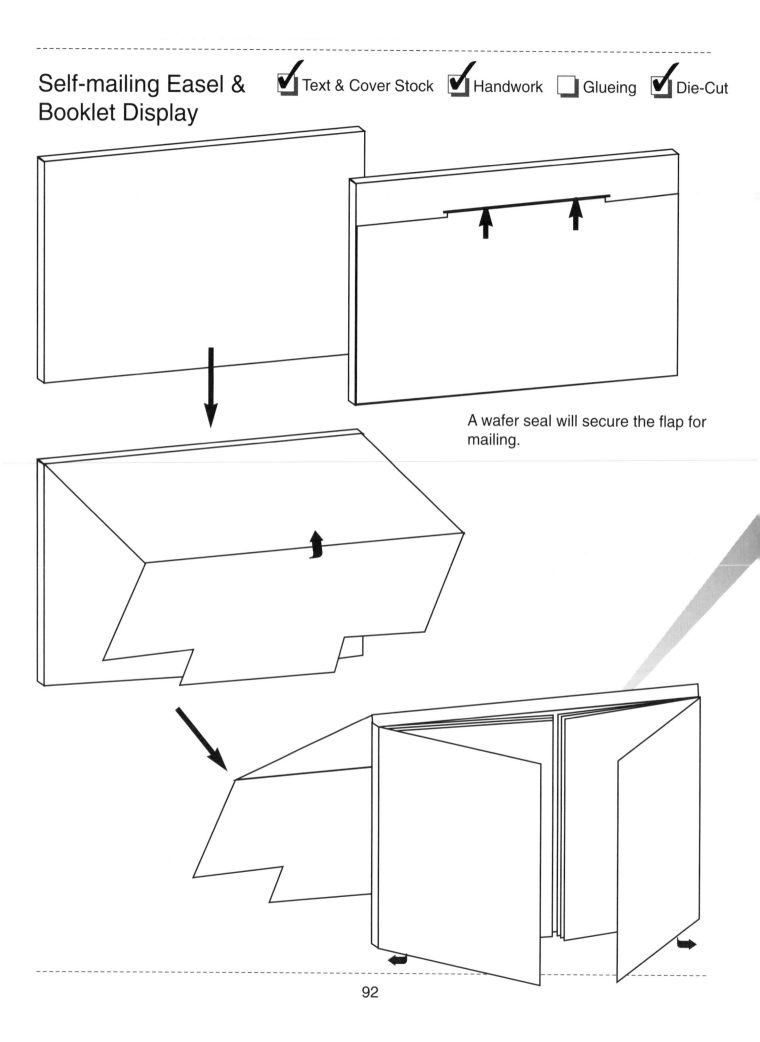

A wafer seal will secure the flap for mailing.

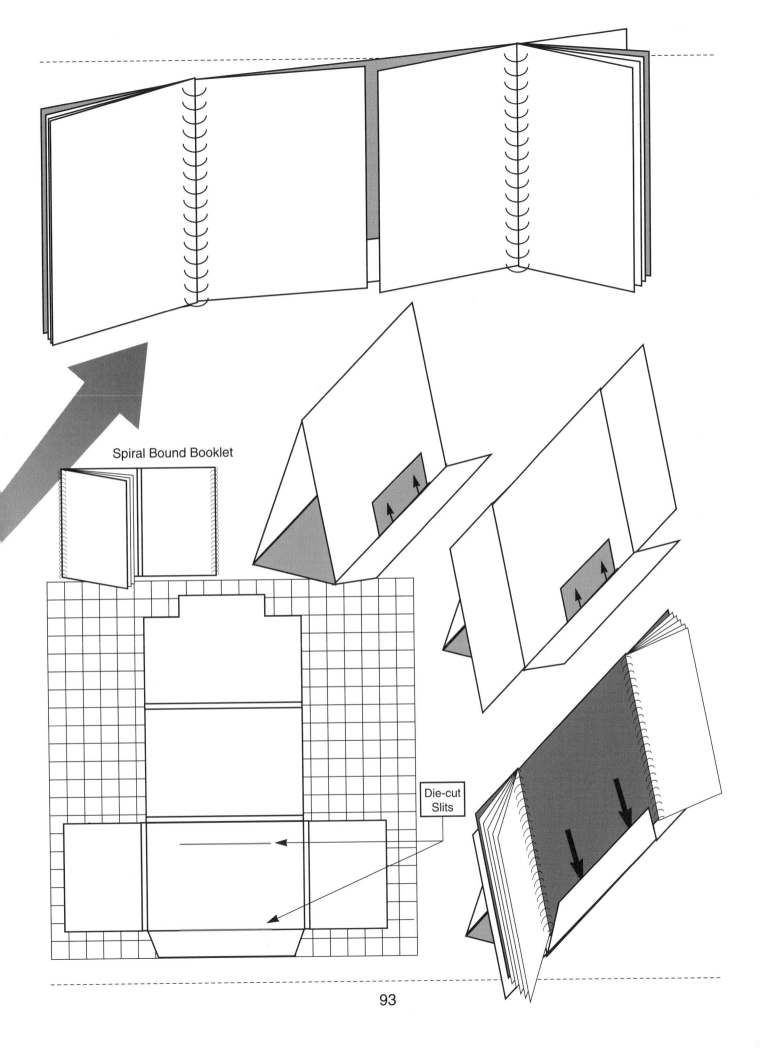

Spiral Bound Booklet

Die-cut Slits

## Pull-Tab Mailer

☑ Cover Stock  ☑ Handwork  ☑ Glueing  ☑ Die-Cut

Pull tab give the recipient the sense that the contents are important.

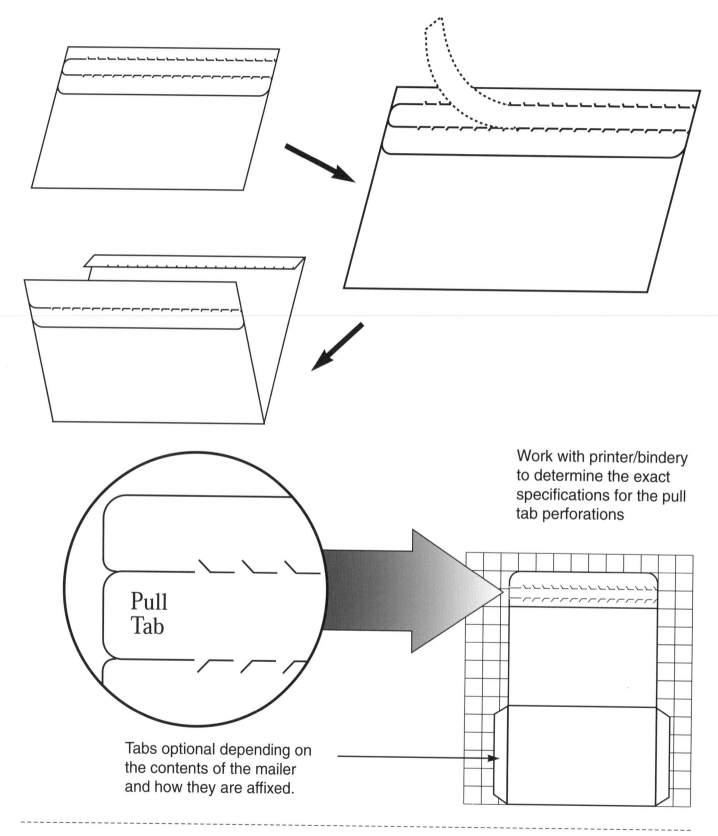

**Pull Tab**

Work with printer/bindery to determine the exact specifications for the pull tab perforations

Tabs optional depending on the contents of the mailer and how they are affixed.

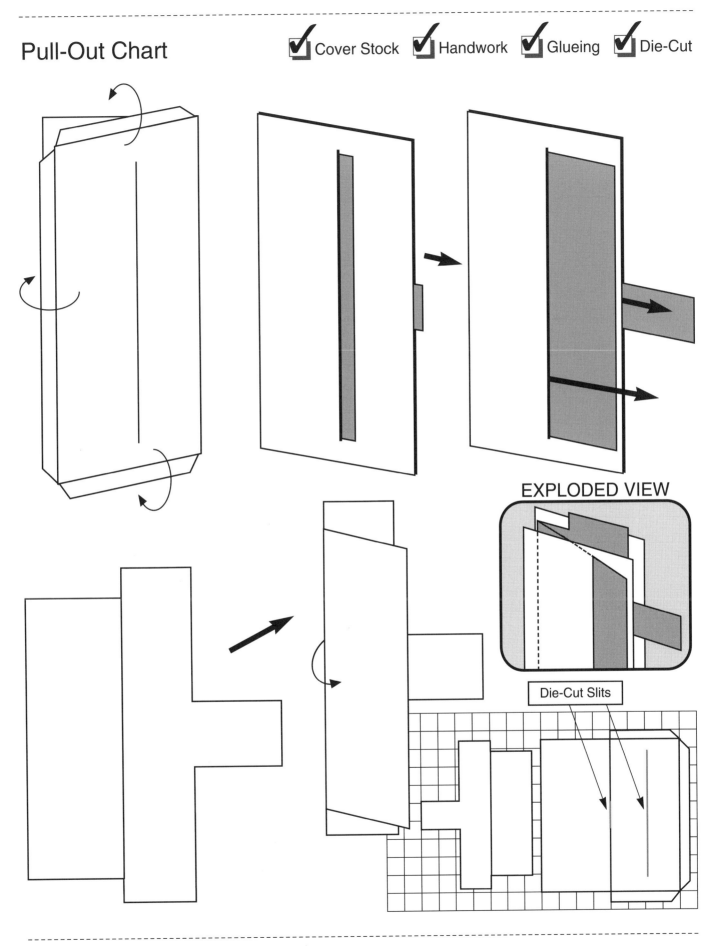

☑ Cover Stock  ☑ Handwork  ☑ Glueing  ☑ Die-Cut

EXPLODED VIEW

Die-Cut Slits

# Tear-Open Mailer

☑ Text & Cover Stock  ☑ Handwork  ☑ Glueing  ☑ Die-Cut

Reveal for special information.

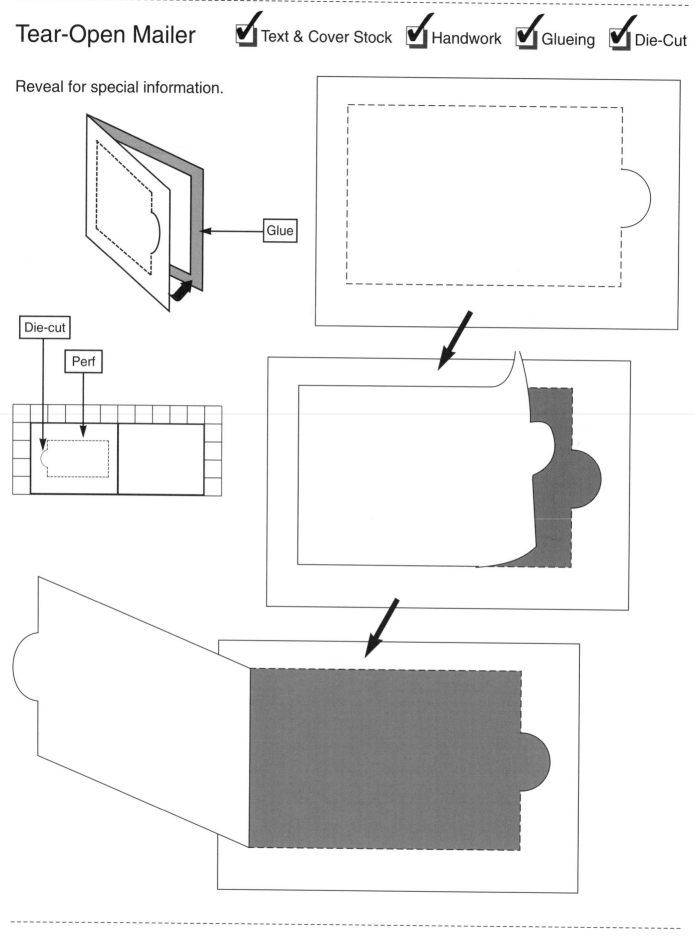

Glue

Die-cut

Perf

## Matchbook Map

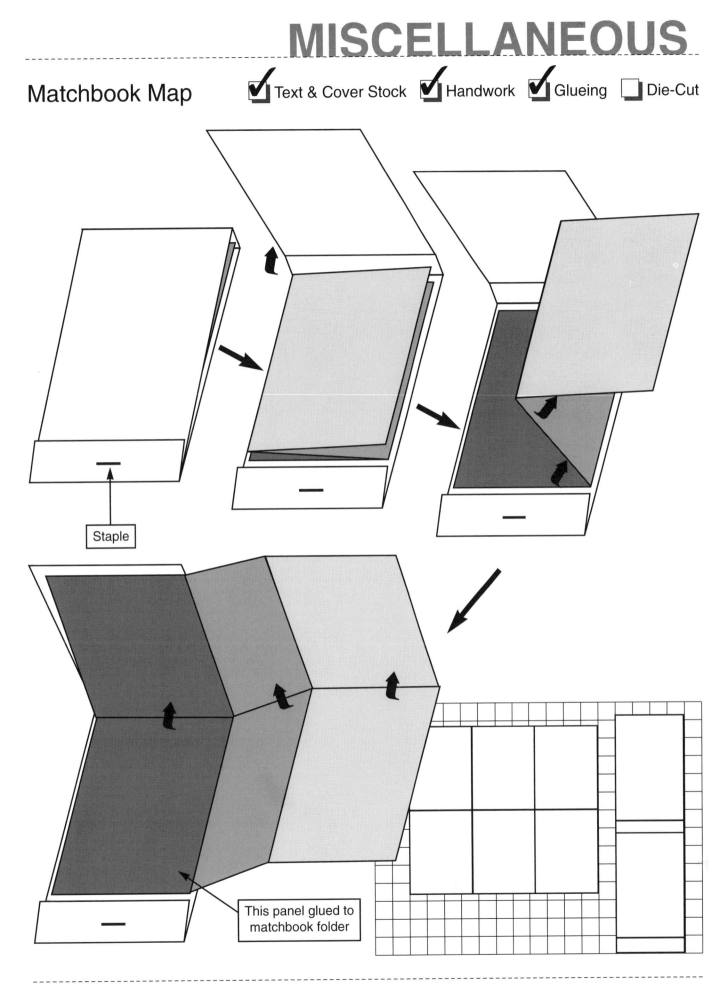

Staple

This panel glued to
matchbook folder

# Paper Swatch (Reveal)

☑ Text Cover Stock ☑ Handwork ☑ Glueing ☑ Die-Cut

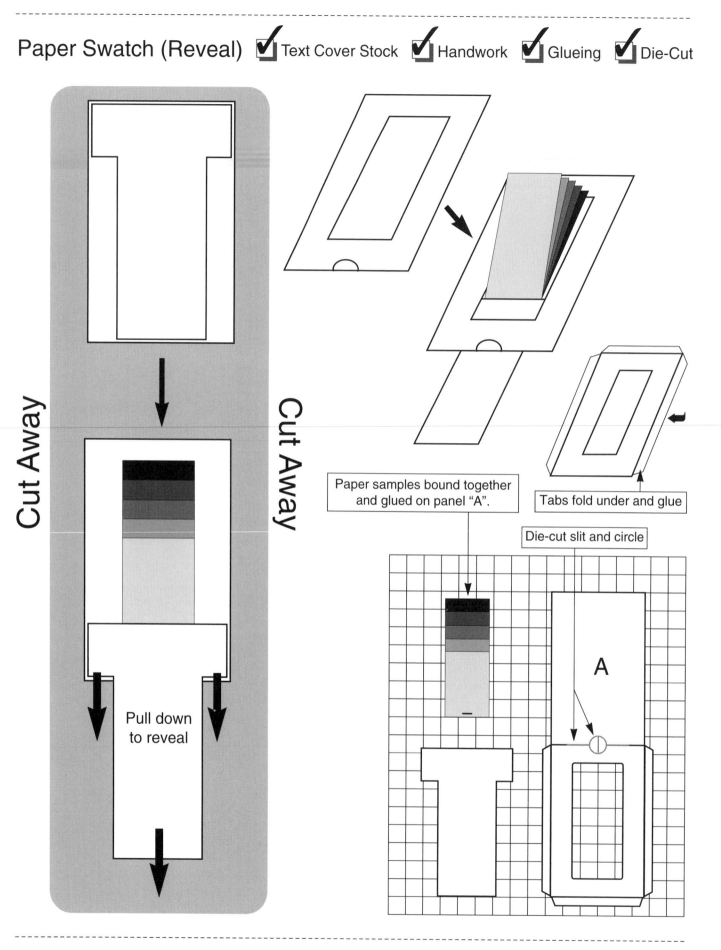

Cut Away

Cut Away

Pull down to reveal

Paper samples bound together and glued on panel "A".

Tabs fold under and glue

Die-cut slit and circle

A

# Self-mailing Booklet with Letter

☑ Text & Cover Stock  ☑ Handwork  ☑ Glueing  ☑ Die-Cut

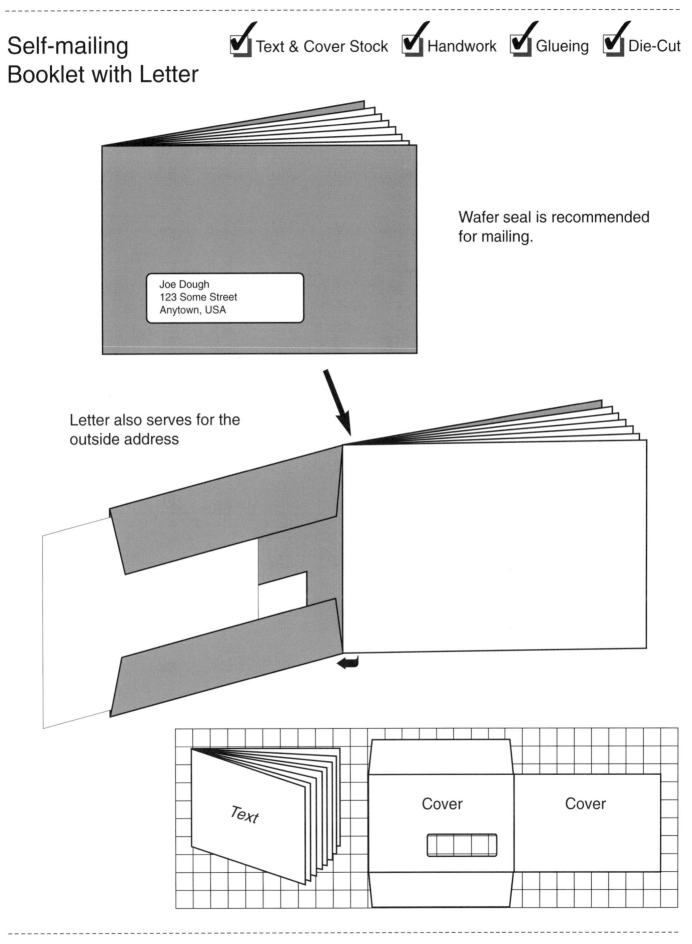

Joe Dough
123 Some Street
Anytown, USA

Wafer seal is recommended for mailing.

Letter also serves for the outside address

Text

Cover

Cover

# One-Piece Return Envelop Mailer

☑ Text or Cover Stock  ☑ Handwork  ☑ Glueing  ☐ Die-Cut

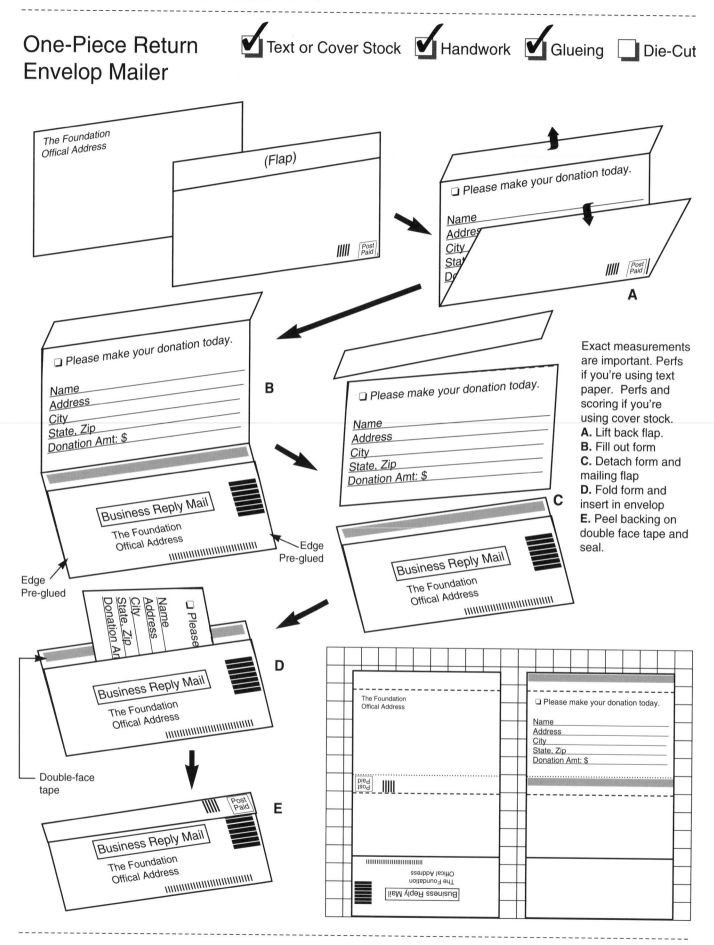

Exact measurements are important. Perfs if you're using text paper. Perfs and scoring if you're using cover stock.

**A.** Lift back flap.
**B.** Fill out form
**C.** Detach form and mailing flap
**D.** Fold form and insert in envelop
**E.** Peel backing on double face tape and seal.

# Wheel Chart

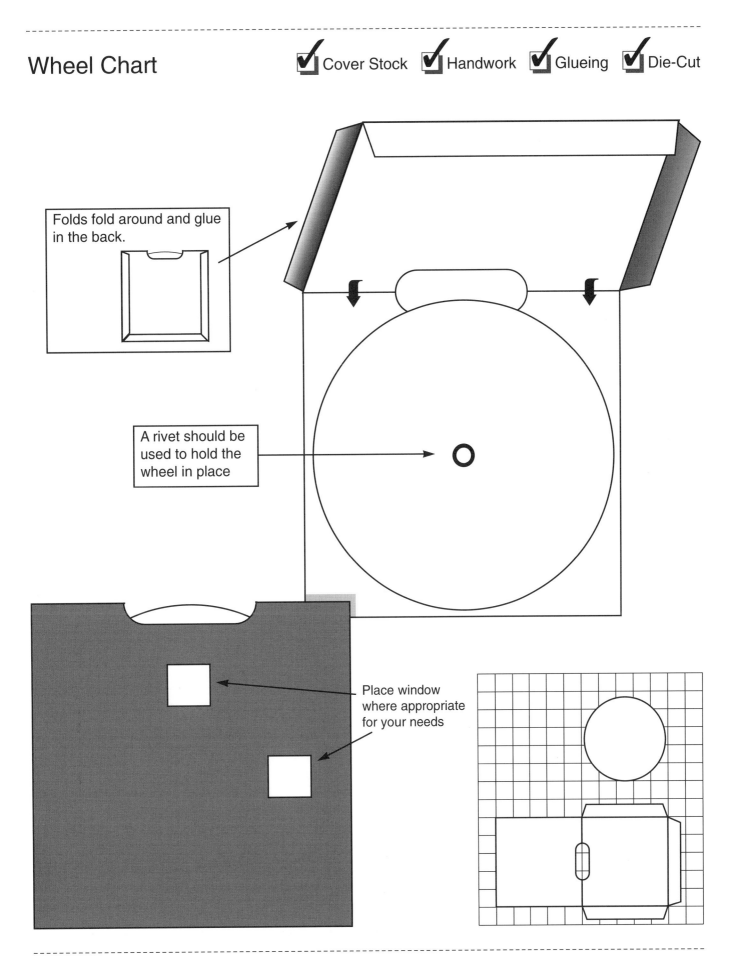

Folds fold around and glue in the back.

A rivet should be used to hold the wheel in place

Place window where appropriate for your needs

# Telescope

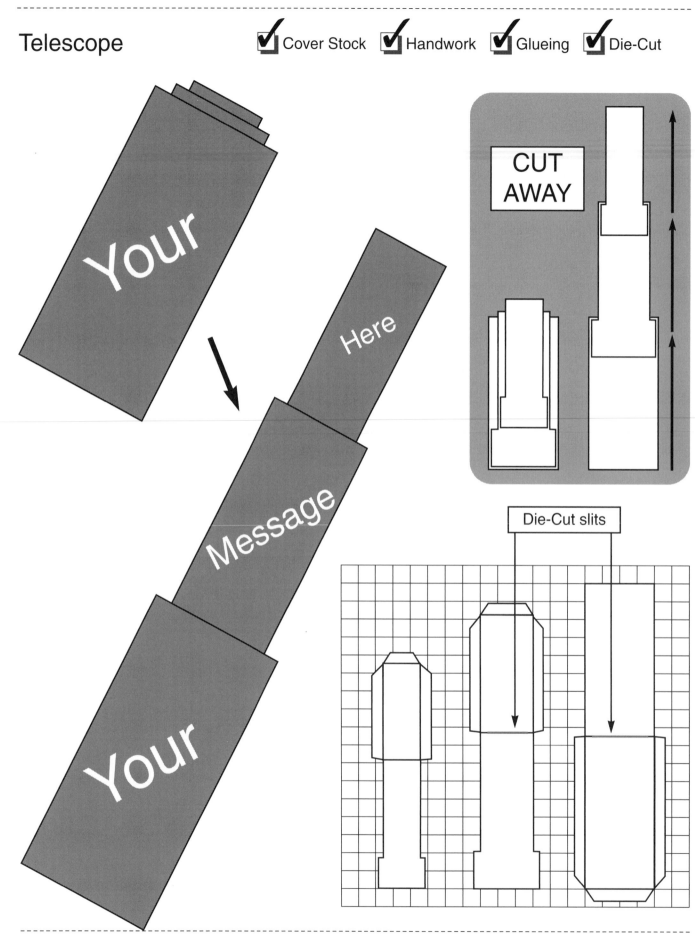

CUT AWAY

Die-Cut slits

# Envelop/Form Combo

☑ Envelop Stock  ☑ Handwork  ☑ Glueing  ☑ Die-Cut

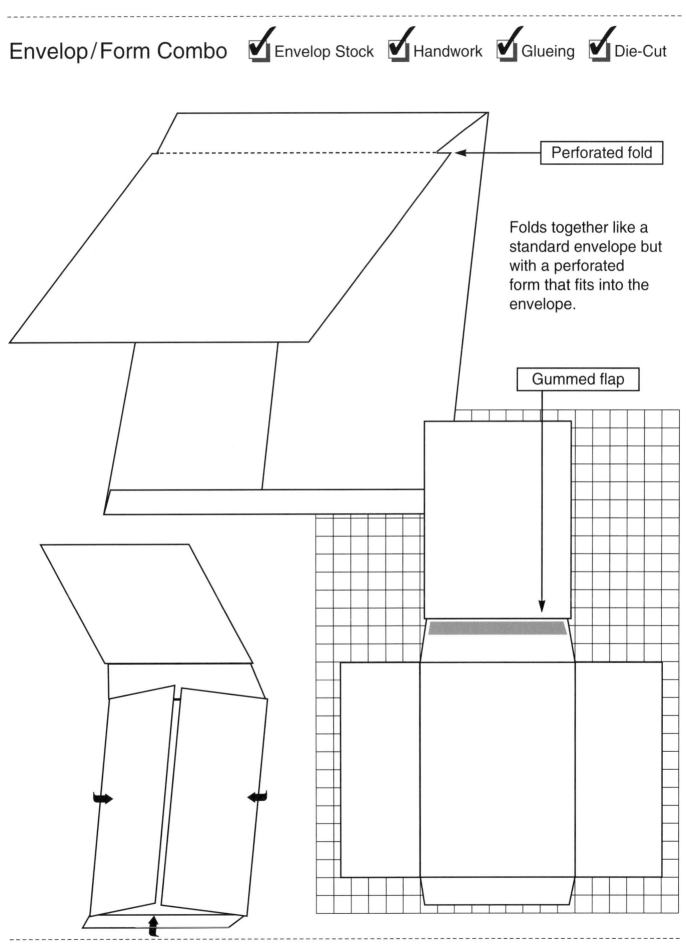

Perforated fold

Folds together like a
standard envelope but
with a perforated
form that fits into the
envelope.

Gummed flap

# Tiered Pop-Up

☑ Cover Stock ☑ Handwork ☑ Glueing ☑ Die-Cut

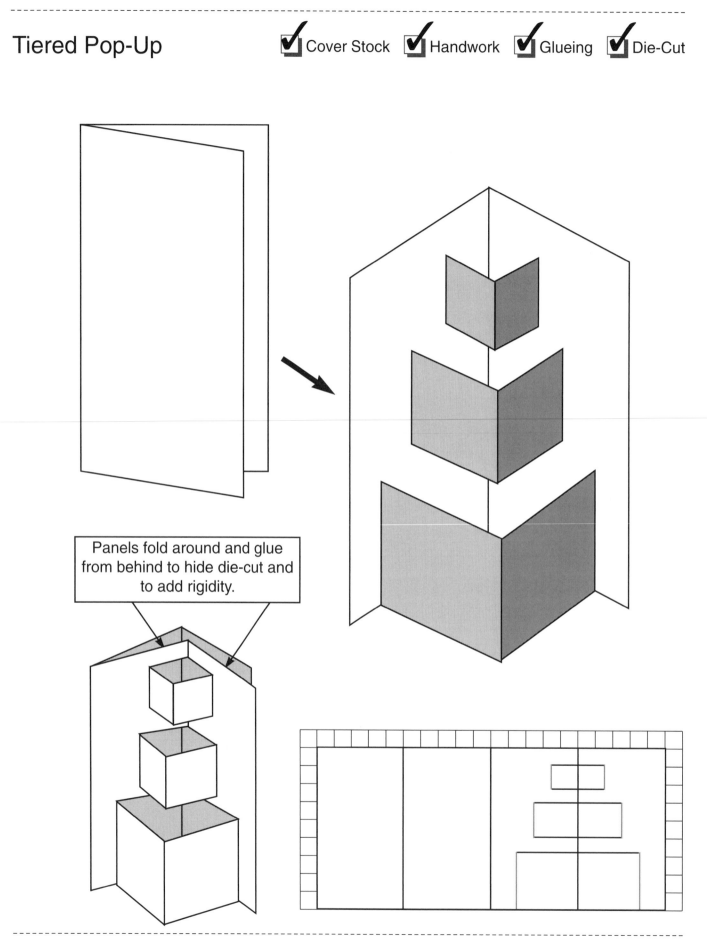

Panels fold around and glue from behind to hide die-cut and to add rigidity.

# Glued-in Pop-up Folder

☑ Cover Stock  ☑ Handwork  ☑ Glueing  ☑ Die-Cut

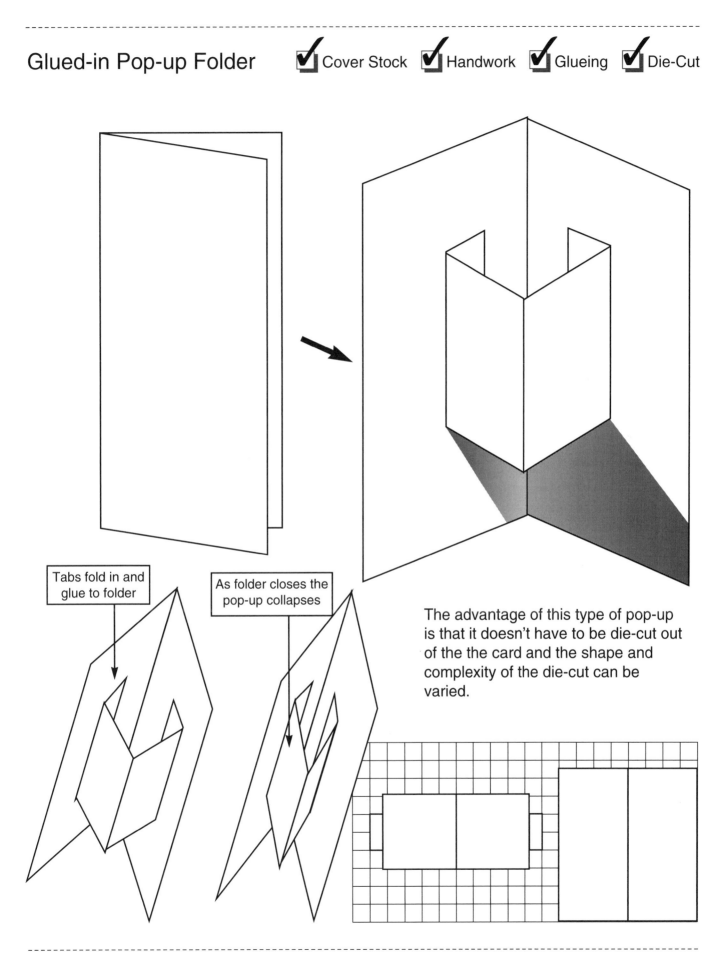

Tabs fold in and glue to folder

As folder closes the pop-up collapses

The advantage of this type of pop-up is that it doesn't have to be die-cut out of the the card and the shape and complexity of the die-cut can be varied.

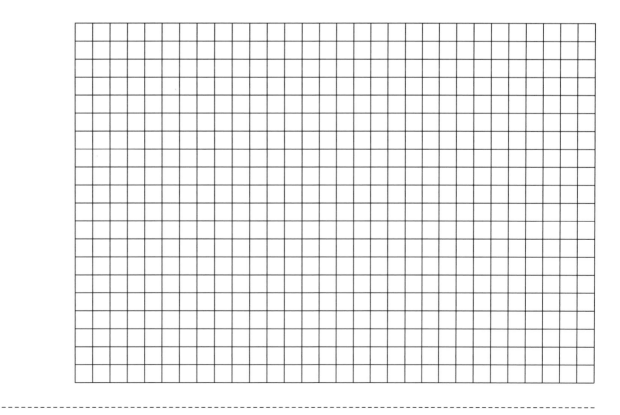

Name_____

☐ Text Stock ☐ Cover Stock ☐ Handwork ☐ Glueing ☐ Taping ☐ Die-Cut

☐ Text Stock  ☐ Cover Stock  ☐ Handwork  ☐ Glueing  ☐ Taping  ☐ Die-Cut

Name_____

☐ Text Stock  ☐ Cover Stock  ☐ Handwork  ☐ Glueing  ☐ Taping  ☐ Die-Cut